ADVANCE PRAISE FOR

PATUXENT INSTITUTION

"Coldren provides a provocative profile and critical analysis of research-based clinical treatment as the mandated marrow of inmate program services at the Patuxent Institution. These research-based programs, surviving through legislative fiat, now provide rare documentation of five decades of the evolving relationship between custody and program staff, the dynamics of juvenile and adult treatment modalities, legislative politics, racial politics, and the ever-compelling community need for services to mentally ill (violent) offenders. This is an essential and valued text for university and law school libraries."

Jess Maghan, Professor and Director,
Forum for Comparative Correction, Chester, Connecticut

PATUXENT INSTITUTION

STUDIES IN CRIME & PUNISHMENT

David A. Schultz and Christina DeJong
General Editors

Vol. 6

PETER LANG
New York • Washington, D.C./Baltimore • Bern
Frankfurt am Main • Berlin • Brussels • Vienna • Oxford

James R. Coldren, Jr.

PATUXENT INSTITUTION

An American Experiment in Corrections

PETER LANG
New York • Washington, D.C./Baltimore • Bern
Frankfurt am Main • Berlin • Brussels • Vienna • Oxford

Library of Congress Cataloging-in-Publication Data

Coldren, James R.
Patuxent Institution: an American experiment in corrections / James R. Coldren, Jr.
p. cm. — (Studies in crime and punishment; vol. 6)
Includes bibliographical references.
1. Patuxent Institution (Md.) 2. Prisons—Maryland—Jessup.
3. Criminals—Rehabiliation—Maryland—Jessup. I. Title. II. Series.
HV9475.M32 P295 365'.975281—dc21 2001038813
ISBN 0-8204-5767-1
ISSN 1529-2444

Bibliographic information published by **Die Deutsche Bibliothek**.
Die Deutsche Bibliothek lists this publication in the "Deutsche Nationalbibliografie"; detailed bibliographic data is available on the Internet at http://dnb.ddb.de/.

Cover design by Sophie Boorsch Appel

275 Seventh Avenue, 28th Floor, New York, NY 10001
www.peterlangusa.com

This book is dedicated to the memory of
Professor Norval Morris.

1923–2004

Table of Contents

Tables

Foreword

This book is the product of a rare combination of skills in its author, James Coldren, the President of the John Howard Association for Prison Reform. He is a leading academic criminologist who also has had substantial experience working in and rising to an administrative position in a prison for high risk offenders. Such a joinder of theory and practice is far from common.

And the prison that is the subject of this book, Patuxent Institution, is an excellent vehicle for his analysis. It too is a rarity. For fifty years it has stood as the one American prison whose purpose is expressly the rehabilitation of longer-term prisoners with "treatment" the leading motif. It has European models in Herstedvester in Denmark and Grendon Underwood in England, but none in the United States. All these institutions employ psychiatric, psychological, sociological and social work staff with the aim of assisting the prisoner to develop himself to the point that he can live safely and productively in the community.

Coldren's book analyzes the organizational and political history and realities of such an endeavor. He does not trumpet success with recidivist data, knowing their appalling fallibility. And, given the media's affection for such recidivist statistics and the legislator's reliance on them, that deserves comment even in a preface.

Recidivist claims usually add together incompatible statistics into a generally uninformative figure. First-, second- and third-time prisoners have very different outcomes. Murderers differ from thieves. Different types of offenders have very different outcomes. Prisoners whose families maintain interest in and support of them on release have very different outcomes from those who have shaken off any family support. And so on with the complex mix of personalities and characters that makes up the prison community; and, indeed, the community at large. Gross recidivist statistics designed to show "what works" are a fraud and in some cases detract us from more subtle questions about correctional effectiveness. To put it less bluntly: a sufficient nosology of treatment outcomes has not yet been developed in criminology.

This is an important book for anyone who realizes just how bad American imprisonment policies have become and is interested how a very difficult group of prisoners can be sensibly handled.

Patuxent's political history and changing organizational structures, told precisely and well, is a substantial contribution to our understanding the realities and potentialities of a treatment-oriented prison.

Patuxent has survived many legal assaults on its structure (some entirely valid) but it has adapted and survived and maintained its original worthy rehabilitative purpose. It is a minor miracle in a depressing landscape.

Norval Morris
Chicago
June 2003

Preface

Rehabilitation — the correction of offenders' behavior — remains a key dilemma in public safety. After over a century of research and practice in corrections, we still struggle with sentencing and the re-integration of ex-offenders into our communities (into labor markets, educational systems, families, and other social networks). In addition, we still engage in the practice of civil commitment for dangerous ex-offenders who have served out their prison sentences. Laws providing for civil commitment of sex offenders, sexual predators or sexually dangerous persons, following successful completion of court-imposed prison sentences, serve as one example of this practice (ACLU 2001, Gabriele 1998, Matson & Lieb 1997). How do we square rehabilitation with retribution and deterrence? How do we know when rehabilitation works? If rehabilitation works, who deserves it? In seeking answers to these questions, our scientific nature often leads us to broad, theoretical works on punishment and society (see, for example, Blumstein & Cohen 1973, Feeley & Simon 1992, Foucault 1977, Garland 1990, 2001, Morris 1974), and appropriately so.

Rarely, however, do the issues that concern us the most about punishment and rehabilitation in America become more salient and tangible when we examine a real case study involving the dual perspectives of psychiatry and the law. In psychiatry (and the related disciplines of psychology, social psychology, and clinical social work) we discover the way we think about treatment of mental illness and related social problems, including crime. In the law (and various legal institutions like the police, courts, and prisons) we discover the way we think about public safety, social control, and correcting behavior. These perspectives are not in opposition to each other. They do at times, however, suggest different approaches to solving the problem of crime.

We play out and observe the interactions of these two giant social institutions in the everyday workings of our criminal justice system — in the ways we educate and train justice system professionals, in police encounters with youth, in diversion practices of various kinds, and in the American prisons and jails that house over two million people every day (Harrison & Beck 2003).

Nowhere in America over the past 50 years has the interaction (and tension) between psychiatry and the law played out in a more fascinating way than it has at Patuxent Institution in Jessup, Maryland. In Patuxent Institution we find the hopes and dreams of a reform-minded judiciary pitted against (and often in collaboration with) the hard-nosed reality of day-to-day confinement and treatment in a maximum security prison.

Now, as our country turns a very serious eye toward community re-entry and re-integration for hundreds of thousands of ex-offenders (many of whom have served long prison sentences) into our communities (Lynch & Sabol 2001, Mukamal 2001, Petersilia 1999, Travis 2000, Travis, Solomon, & Waul 2001), the lessons learned through the Patuxent experience become very valuable indeed. Recidivism statistics aside, we need to know how treatment happens (and can flourish) inside restrictive prison settings, how the prison organization is affected by the integration of treatment into the daily regimen, what it takes to sustain such initiatives, as well as the social and political processes that shape and influence rehabilitation practices within corrections.

This book takes a very close look at Patuxent Institution, the one prison in America that has a legislative mandate to provide a daily regimen of research-based and clinically appropriate treatment to violent and mentally ill offenders, in a restrictive (e.g., maximum security) environment. Amazingly, Patuxent Institution has been practicing correctional treatment this way since the mid-1950s. Equally amazing is how little is known about Patuxent. Descriptive studies, investigative reports, and statistical reports have been written about Patuxent, and there have been several evaluative studies. Our concern in this book is not what Patuxent has done, per se, or how well it has performed (the "what works" question); rather our concern here is the organizational adaptation and political survival of a correctional institution that bucks the trends. If rehabilitation is questioned (or, more often, rejected) as the key goal for prisons in America, then why does Patuxent exist, and how has it managed to exist for all these years when key social and governmental institutions like the press, the legislature, and hard-line conservatives, to mention a few, reject its premise and often work to undermine or eliminate it?

The answer to this question, developed through a historical and political analysis of Patuxent's survival as a public organization, helps us understand prisons as organizations, and helps us understand how prison staff and administrators manage the day-to-day and month-to-month organizational challenges that are unique to correctional institutions.

Acknowledgments

Many past and present employees at Patuxent deserve thanks for their encouragement and support over the years that I worked at Patuxent Institution and while I worked on this project. Dr. Norma Gluckstern, former Director of Patuxent Institution, opened Patuxent's gates to me and in doing so opened the doors to the real world of corrections. Without her confidence in me this story would never have been told. Former Director Richard Rosenblatt and then Associate Director (now Director) Randall Nero, Ph.D. were kind enough to open the gates to Patuxent once again, allowing my second visit in August 2001. Dr. Richard Craig, Patuxent's Director of Research during my second visit, was helpful in coordinating a week-long visit to Patuxent. Without the trust and assistance of these individuals, this book would not have been possible. Thanks to the staff and inmates at Patuxent who took time out of their days to talk with me or allow me to observe a small part of their lives. I greatly value their many contributions, great and small, to this research.

Laura Kunard deserves special mention for her help in making preparations for this book. Dr. Michael Reisig of Michigan State University deserves a special note of thanks for encouraging me to turn my doctoral thesis into this book.

The staff and Board of Directors at the John Howard Association were very gracious in allowing me the time to finish this project.

Finally, I thank my entire family (immediate and extended) for their encouragement over the past few years and for providing me the time to work on this research.

The author gratefully acknowledges permission to reprint granted by Alan M. Wilner and Pauline H. Menes for excerpts from interviews with them, and Francis Carney for permission to reprint excerpts from his unpublished manuscript *The Will to Fail,* 1985, and from *Criminality and Its Treatment,* R.E. Krieger, ©1989.

Chapter One

Introduction

Once established institutions become suspect,
the curiosity of historians is immediately stimulated.
The Oxford History of the Prison, 1995, p. ix

Patuxent Institution, a maximum-security prison located in Jessup, Maryland, 15 miles south of the city of Baltimore, is the nation's most intriguing and most experimental prison. Little is known about Patuxent, however, save what the Maryland state government prints in its annual reports, published almost yearly since the mid-1950s. Patuxent has been called the nation's most sued correctional facility (Carney 1985, 4). At one point in the mid-1960s, Patuxent Institution was named in 156 actions brought to the courts by 119 individuals (Roy, circa 1986, p. 5).

In years past, Patuxent was a prison where offenders could be sent by the courts with indeterminate sentences, to be released when the prison treatment staff determined it was safe to send them back to society, even if that meant they would stay in prison past the length of the sentence handed down by the courts. This actually happened in only a few instances, but the prospect of such a sentence, coupled with a lack of information about how the prison operated, created a state of fear, ignorance, and uncertainty for justice and legal system professionals as well as inmates and their families, that eventually became intolerable.

In 1976, the law authorizing Patuxent's existence and practices changed, and Patuxent Institution became what it is today—a prison that inmates volunteer for,[1] where treatment programs are available and the hope of rehabilitation exists. Patuxent has changed in significant ways since 1976. Its programs have changed and the inmates admitted to the treatment program have changed. It now houses both male and female adult inmates, as well as incarcerated youths of both genders. It offers mental health programming for inmates preparing to go back to society, or to go back to the regular prison population after a mental health crisis. It offers drug treatment programs, and it offers educational programs ranging from traditional schooling to keyboarding classes to horticulture classes.

Patuxent is unique in other important ways. Patuxent operates its own correctional system, with its own admissions, inmate review, and paroling functions separate from the Division of Correction[2] (DOC) in Maryland. Both Patuxent and the DOC exist side-by-side within the Maryland Department of Public Safety and Correctional Services, and significant links exist between the two systems, but Patuxent operates independently, with a different mission, different resources, and a different approach to the business of inmate correction.

I joined the Patuxent staff in 1984, with a master's degree in Sociology and a desire to experience criminal justice from the operational, practitioner perspective. I had just moved to Maryland from Chicago, and heard of Patuxent through the local news and through professional colleagues. Nothing could have prepared me for the experience I had working for three years as an administrative assistant to the Director of Patuxent.[3] It was as challenging and rewarding as it was frustrating. I cut my eyeteeth as a criminal justice professional there, and learned as many professional and life lessons during those three years as I have in the 15 years since I left. I did not enter Patuxent with the idea of making it the topic of my doctoral work. It was not until later, just after I left to take another position in Washington, DC, that I decided to conduct my doctoral research at Patuxent. So I returned, occasionally, as an outside researcher and collected the information to write the doctoral thesis that is now this book. I returned, briefly, in the summer of 2001 to revisit Patuxent and update my understanding of institutional operations and programs.

One might expect the focus of a book on a prison like Patuxent Institution to focus on the instrumental question—does it work? Does Patuxent rehabilitate violent convicted offenders? Does it do so better than other prisons? Does it cost more than other prisons? What is the recidivism rate at Patuxent? Indeed, these questions occupied a good portion of my time and energy when I worked there, since I was Patuxent's first full-time Director of Research. However, it was my observation that the answers to those questions didn't always matter much to those whose business it was to know about Patuxent. Historically, no matter how Patuxent "performed" (and at times it performed poorly, or at least seemed to), or how little those who controlled Patuxent's future knew about what really happened behind the walls of the prison, Patuxent continued to exist with few changes to its main objective—treating and rehabilitating violent convicted offenders with mental health or emotional problems. Thus, I developed a different research question—not how well does Patuxent do, but why does it exist?

We tend to view prisons as monolithic, unchanging organizations, rather than as dynamic, multi-faceted organizations with the range of concerns, challenges, and experiences that other, more visible, organizations encounter. However, if we want to understand prisons, and if we want to change them in any way, we must change this perspective. Prisons, as complex, contradictory, and at times brutal organizations go through change cycles, crises in legitimacy and political struggles of various kinds, all influenced by actors within the organization, actors in the environment, social and institutional forces, and by economic contingencies. Once we understand these phenomena better as they relate to prisons, then we will be in a better position to effect change in prison organizations.

This book examines the history and development of Patuxent Institution, as well as the adaptive behavior of the organization, which has survived the conservative trend in politics and the administration of criminal justice over the last several decades. A prison as a public organization receives legitimacy from the society that surrounds it and more directly from the political bodies in its immediate external environment. In fact, it receives perhaps the most legitimacy from the legislature that appropriates its funds, presumeably in the public interest. If Patuxent Institution exists as a treatment providing prison, as the following paragraphs describe, how has it managed to survive when the general public, the political climate, and its legislature question rehabilitation as a legitimate goal for a prison?[4]

In one sense, Patuxent is an anomaly, an irregular or chance occurrence among prisons in this conservative era, or in any era. On the other hand, Patuxent's long history of conflict and confrontation with the public and legislature, and the fact that it still exists as an innovative correctional institution, suggest that we look for another explanation. As one of the most controversial prisons in America's history, Patuxent fought and survived several major legal and legitimacy battles in its time.

The question of Patuxent's survival and adaptation touches on many aspects of the sociology of complex organizations: organization creation, development, structure, and culture; organization environment, and organization-environment interactions; adaptive strategies; institutionalization; the political economy of public organizations; and external influences on organizations. This research examines these issues for the case of Patuxent Institution and answers questions regarding how adaptive mechanisms operate to insure survival for a public organization such as Patuxent. Following is a brief historical and organizational sketch of Patuxent, followed by a review of relevant literature in organization and prison studies, thus grounding this research in current and past research and theories about the adaptive behavior of prisons and other complex public organizations.

Patuxent Institution opened its doors in 1955 as a model for the development and application of psychiatry with dangerous criminals, and it still operates, almost 50 years later, as a therapeutic prison.

When it opened, Patuxent Institution comprised one building with a capacity for approximately 200 inmates. It was as much a product of the Maryland judiciary's dissatisfaction with treatment options for offenders deemed legally sane but clinically severely mentally disturbed, as it was an "enlightened" approach to psychological positivism (Reiblich and Hubbard 1950, 1; Lejins 1977). Under its original enabling legislation, Article 31-B of the Public General Laws of Maryland, Patuxent operated within the Maryland Division of Correction as a facility for the humane confinement of "Defective Delinquents" serving indeterminate sentences. Defective Delinquents were individuals who demonstrated "persistent aggravated antisocial or criminal behavior," related to intellectual deficiency or emotional disorder (Reiblich and Hubbard 1950, 31).

Patuxent clinical staff (originally psychologists and psychiatrists,clinical social workers came later) evaluated inmates referred to the Institution by the courts, and could recommend indefinite confinement through a civil proceeding with a jury or panel of judges. A finding of defective delinquency by the court resulted in suspension of the original criminal sentence and confinement at Patuxent Institution until the professional staff felt the individual no longer presented a danger to society. Commitment to Patuxent meant an indeterminate sentence—admission with no approximate or estimated release date, only with the knowledge that participation and success in treatment should bring about a recommendation by Patuxent that the court release the inmate from his sentence.[5] Patuxent's enabling legislation provided avenues for review of a finding of defective delinquency, which may have resulted in release from Patuxent, but there was no fixed sentence, nor was there a sentence range (minimum-maximum). Under its original mandate and procedures, inmates could be kept in confinement at Patuxent longer than their criminal sentence would have kept them incarcerated.

Treatment at Patuxent consisted of an integrated program of individual and/or group therapy, education, and vocational shops in a graded tier[6] system. An Institutional Board of Review, comprised of members from Patuxent's administration and from the outside community, acted as the paroling authority. In later years, as the inmate population grew, the unit treatment team approach was introduced. Inmates were assigned to one of four treatment teams, each consisting of social workers, psychologists, and psychiatrists.

Almost from its inception, Patuxent operated amidst local and national controversy. Many legal, public, and administrative battles were waged around the Institution. The principal controversies revolved around the indeterminate sentence, coercive therapy, prediction of dangerousness, cost effectiveness, and procedural matters regarding defective delinquency determinations. One court case reached the United States Supreme Court (*McNeil v. Director*) concerning the right to hold inmates at Patuxent who refused psychiatric examination. The Court decided in favor of the inmate, prompting the release of 44 "refusers" in October 1972. In that same case, the Supreme Court did not rule on the constitutionality of the defective delinquency law since the petitioners named no longer resided at Patuxent (Carney 1985, 151–159).

In 1960, an amendment to Article 31-B moved Patuxent out from under the Division of Correction, establishing it as an independent prison. Controversy continued throughout the 1960s and reached its peak in the early to mid-1970s. The mounting public and political pressure culminated in a revision of Article 31-B in 1977, into the "Eligible Person" statute.

Patuxent now operates with an average daily population of approximately 832.[7] The Institution's Board of Review continues to review the progress of inmates in Patuxent treatment programs. As noted above, Patuxent is a "total correctional facility," separate from Maryland's Division of Correction (DOC) and with control over its own admission, classification and parole and release decisions.[8] Patuxent houses and treats several special classes of offenders. These include approximately 350[9] adult male, adult female, and youth Eligible Persons (EPs), defined by law[10] as a person who:

(1) has been convicted of a crime and is serving a sentence of imprisonment with at least three years remaining to be served,

(2) has an intellectual impairment or emotional unbalance,

(3) is likely to respond favorably to the programs and services provided at Patuxent Institution, and

(4) is better able to respond to remediation through Patuxent Institution's programs and services than by other incarceration.

Individuals may not be found eligible for Patuxent if they are:

- serving two or more life sentences,
- serving one or more life sentences in which a jury found one or more aggravating circumstances existed, or
- convicted of first degree murder, first degree rape, or a first degree sex offense (unless at the time of sentencing the judge recommends a referral to Patuxent for evaluation).

Special conditions regarding youth eligibility for Patuxent include:

- must be under the age of 21 years,

- must be referred to Patuxent by the court at the time of sentencing,
- must have received a sentence of at least three years, and
- must be deemed amenable to treatment in the program (Patuxent Institution 2000, 15).

Patuxent also houses almost 250 inmates in several special treatment programs—approximately 200 in a program for DOC inmates who have experienced acute mental health problems (with an additional 30 to 40 in a "step-down" unit linked to this one for those preparing for release from the mental health unit), and another 90 in a drug treatment program.

The Maryland legislature originally created Patuxent Institution with public protection stated as its first priority, and rehabilitation as its second (Reiblich and Hubbard 1950, 2; Carney 1985, v, 5). This priority ranking of the Institution's goals still applies (though the current legislation refers to "remediation," not "rehabilitation"), but a prison in the hands of behavioral scientists will not operate in the same manner as a prison in the hands of correctional administrators.[11] Historically, rehabilitation at Patuxent was never relegated to a minor or insignificant role, and the treatment approach (therapy, education, and vocational training integrated with a behavioral modification program and control of parole decisions) changed little over the years. As the law now stands, almost any inmate in the Maryland Division of Correction may volunteer to participate in Patuxent's program, and will typically be placed in a queue of applicants for admission (a three- to six-month waiting period). Patuxent's evaluation team, comprised of at least three behavioral science professionals (psychiatrist, psychologist, social worker) admits approximately 50 percent of the inmate applicants based on its judgment of "treatability" or "parolability" (Patuxent Institution 2000, 16).

Treatment for inmates in the Eligible Person program(s) consists of weekly psychotherapy in small groups of 10 to 15 inmates, conducted by trained professionals and larger sessions of "tier" counseling with 30 to 35 inmates and five to seven professional staff. The treatment program integrates therapy with more traditional educational, vocational, recreation, and social services in a graded tier system. Newly admitted inmates begin on Level One, with minimum privileges, and progress to Level Four with maximum privileges. The professional staff monitors inmates' progress and promotes or demotes them in the level system. Insufficient program participation and lack of motivation for treatment (or excessive violent or unruly behavior) may result in return of the inmate to the Division of Correction.

The Board of Review, Patuxent's paroling authority, monitors each inmate's progress annually at a minimum (reviewing approximately 30 inmates per month). Based on the recommendation of the professional staff, it may grant leave "status" to an inmate (with approval from the Office of the Secretary of Public Safety and Correctional Services), marking the beginning of a gradual monitored leave (day release) program which leads to work release and eventually to parole. The Board of Review consists of four Patuxent professional staff (the Director, two Associate Directors, and the custodial Warden) and five citizen members appointed by the Governor (one of whom must be a member of a victim's rights organization). The Board of Review decides most cases by simple majority vote (some decisions require a "supermajority," 7 of 9 "yes" votes by Board members). Since about 1990, a separate Citizens Review Board (appointed by the Governor) has served as a monitoring and oversight body, meeting several times a year with Patuxent staff and administrators, monitoring Patuxent's compliance with inmate release and victim notification procedures.

Over the years Patuxent Institution survived several organized public and legislative efforts to abolish it or subsume the organization once again under the Division of Correction. Patuxent's survival over more than five decades that have witnessed major changes in the fields of penology and administration of justice, changes that perhaps militate against its survival, suggest the principal question for this research—How does Patuxent Institution survive as a rehabilitation-oriented prison, especially in light of (1) conservatism in the administration of justice and criticism of the medical model in corrections since the mid-1970s, (2) increasing reliance over several decades on incarceration as a crime prevention and crime control tactic (resulting in crowded prisons and, arguably, less tolerance for a place like Patuxent), and (3) criticisms of the Institution in the state of Maryland?

This historical case study of Patuxent Institution explores this question and its numerous attendant sub-questions. Interviews with past and present Patuxent employees and with significant actors outside of the Institution provide rich detail concerning bona fide threats to the Institution's legitimacy, as well as its history, organizational culture, and operations. Archival material from many sources of information about Patuxent (institutional files, newspapers, legislative information, past writings on Patuxent) supplement the interview data. The author's personal experience as an employee of Patuxent with access to high level decision making meetings and materials during three years of employment there provide additional "insider" information.

We begin with a literature review covering the key themes of this research: organizational adaptation, and prisons in society. Next we present the history of Patuxent Institution, paying particular attention to the organization's external environment and several survival and legitimacy threats. We then focus on several of Patuxent's most compelling survival-threatening experiences—looking at the key actors involved in the Institution's most troublesome times, dominant coalitions on both or all sides of the issues, decisions made and final outcomes for the organization. The final chapters analyze the survival-threatening situations for Patuxent and discuss the implications the findings have for current organizational theory. A special epilogue (added recently to update the reader on Patuxent's current operations and status), reconsiders legitimacy issues for Patuxent 10 years after the original research for this book was completed.

Notes

1. In fact, under current law, youth offenders can be sent to Patuxent involuntarily, at the discretion of the sentencing judge and within certain legal parameters.

2. Throughout this book, we use the name "Division of Correction" or DOC to refer to main correctional system in Maryland within the Division of Public Safety and Correctional Services, though it has been given different names over the years.

3. Norma Gluckstern, Ed.D. was the Director of Patuxent during my tenure there, from 1984 to 1987. At the time she was the only, and first ever, female director of an all-male maximum-security prison in America. Technically, Patuxent has a warden, the chief custodial officer, who serves under the Director.

4. At the time of this writing, societal concern over the issue of offender reentry was at an all-time high compared to the past several decades. Rehabilitation, then, has become somewhat more "legitimized" due to several factors (including the federal government's acknowledgment of the reentry issue, and the availability of federal funding in various forms to promote safe community reentry for returning ex-offenders). This does not alter the fact that Patuxent Institution remains as this country's longest standing investment in violent offender rehabilitation based on a clinical treatment model.

5. Females were not admitted into Patuxent until 1986.

6. In Patuxent's graded tier system (then and now), inmates begin their prison stay under restricted living conditions with few privileges and, as they exhibit acceptable behavior (infraction-free, participation in programs), they move up into more open, lenient living quarters with more privileges. For rule-breaking behavior, or insufficient participation in programs, they may be demoted to lower tiers, and they may be removed from the Institution and sent back to the general inmate population.

7. This figure provided by Patuxent Institution (communication from Dr. Randall Nero, July 7, 2003). At the close of Fiscal Year 1990, Patuxent's average daily population was 875 (Patuxent Institution 1990, 29).

8. In 1989 the Maryland legislature acted to curtail the control exercised by the Patuxent administration over admissions and release decisions, by placing restrictions on the types of inmates allowed to enter Patuxent for treatment and by placing final authority for parole decisions in the Office of the Secretary for Public Safety and Correctional Services and in the Governor's office (for inmates serving life sentences). Other restrictions on Patuxent's paroling authority were legislated in later years. In addition, Patuxent now operates a youth eligible person program, admission to which is controlled by the courts (e.g., the sentencing judge may send a youth to Patuxent), not by Patuxent.

9. Patuxent's current enabling legislation (see below) limits the number of persons in the eligible person population to 350 (Title 4-202).

10. Until recently, Article 31-B of the Public General Laws of Maryland served as Patuxent's enabling and authorizing legislation. In October 1999, the Maryland Legislature moved Patuxent's law to

Title 4 (Correctional Services) of the Annotated Code of Maryland (§ 4-101).

11. By law, two of Patuxent's four top administrators are psychiatrists or behavioral science professionals.

Chapter Two

Theoretical Framework

In the social sciences theory can direct research or research can inform theory. Optimally, research and theory development continue in cycles, each simultaneously drawing from and guiding the other (Kuhn 1962, Merton 1948). In this analysis, we rely on organizational research and theory to inform the development of a grounded theory (Turner 1981, 1983) of Patuxent Institution's adaptation and survival over almost half a century. Three organizational perspectives come into play in this analysis – the management perspective (leadership determines organizational outcomes), organizational environment and dependency theory (organizational outcomes are the result of ongoing and emergent organization-environment exchanges), and the institutional perspective (organizations exert and react to larger social forces that determine, at least in part, organizational outcomes). Each of these theoretical perspectives, and several other related ones having to do with the particular case of public organizations and the social psychology of organizations, must be taken into account to understand the ongoing adaptation and survival of Patuxent Institution. In this chapter, we review the broad literature on organizational theory and several key studies of public organizations, including prisons, to lay the groundwork for the historical analysis and interpretation of Patuxent's history that follows.

Several theoretical and empirical works in the sociology of organizations provide the foundation for this study of Patuxent Institution, beginning with the writings of social theorists and penologists in the late 1950s and continuing to the present. This literature helps identify the societal and organizational phenomena that must be studied to gain an understanding of the adaptation and survival of a correctional institution like Patuxent over many years.

Our theoretical overview begins with the open systems perspective of Parsons' (1956, 1965), and March and Simon's (1958) discussion of organizational rationality. It covers subsequent theoretical developments in the sociology of organizations from the works of Thompson (1967) and Selznick (1949), to the more contemporary theories of Pfeffer and Salancik (1978) and others concerning resource dependency and organization-environment relationships. Wamsley and Zald's (1973) work on public organizations and political economy provides the basis for a discussion of Kimberly's key work on environmental influences on the structure of rehabilitation workshops, Kauffman (1976) on the survival of federal organizations, Bowman and Snyder (1985) on the survival of the Selective Service System, and Wilson (1985) on the death of an educational organization. We then consider contributions made by Clemmer (1958), Sykes (1958), Jacobs (1977), Martin and Eckland-Olson (1987), Carney (1989), Garland (1990), Morris and Rothman (1995), and Conover (2000) from their research on prisons from several different perspectives.[1] Finally, a discussion of work by DiMaggio (1991) on organization fields, and Powell and DiMaggio (1991) on neo-institutionalism brings us back to consideration of organizational and institutional theory and what we have learned about Patuxent Institution.

Organization Theory: Development and Implications for the Research

The primary contributions of sociological theory to the study of organizations[2] lies in the natural or open systems perspective, and the concept of uncertainty, found in the work of Parsons, Thompson, Selznick, and others. This perspective considers organizations (as opposed to individuals, small informal groups, or communities) as appropriate units of analysis, and as dynamic social systems that act on, and react to, their external environments. Three concepts from the writings of Talcott Parsons bear directly on the issue of organizational survival: integration and boundary exchanges, power, and levels of hierarchy and control. In some of his work, Parsons examines the integrative functions of organizations. By this he means organizational structure and actions which link the organization to the structure of larger social organizations, or to society. Organizations achieve integration through boundary exchanges, whereby an organization interacts, and actually exchanges goods, services, or resources with other organizations. Organizations must achieve some balance between dependence on and independence from other organizations, and some level of compatibility with other organizations and broader social units in order to survive (Parsons 1956, 80–85). Integration refers also to the linking of smaller social units to the focal organization.

According to Parsons, organizational independence from other organizations is a function of power. Parsons defines power as "...the generalized capacity to mobilize resources in the interests of attainment of a system goal." Power is typically exercised within an organization's realm, but it is tied to external resources because it must be legitimized. Thus, organizational power is dependent on integration and boundary exchanges. An organization must be compatible with its environment in order to exercise power in it (Parsons 1965, 41–44).

Parsons identifies three levels of responsibility and control in organizations: technical, managerial, and institutional. Technical responsibilities tend to be closed (limited) and located among line staff. Institutional responsibilities (e.g., legitimating, goal setting, planning for the future) lie in upper administrative echelons. Managerial responsibilities lie in middle management service functions, and mediate between the technical and institutional levels (Parsons 1965, 60–65). Adaptive strategies (and the power exercised in their use), then, should be found at the middle and upper levels of organizational responsibility. Research by Schwab, Ungson, and Brown suggests that this may depend on organizational type (institutional-type power may be exercised by lower-level staff in decentralized organizations), but their research was limited to private sector organizations (high technology electronics firms and wood products firms) and was not conclusive on this matter (Schwab, Ungson, and Brown 1985, 84–85).

James March and Herbert Simon provide an enlightening perspective on the adaptive behavior of organizations through their discussion of limited rationality in organizations. They modify the Parsonian notion in classical organization theory that organizations (and organizational members) are rational, goal-oriented, and purpose-oriented actors, arguing that the practical limits on human cognition and rationality limit the extent to which people or organizations can act rationally. When faced with decisions and limited, imperfect information, organizational actors tend toward "satisficing" behavior, whereby they choose the available alternative that meets minimum criteria for goal attainment, rather than conducting an exhaustive search of all available options and assessing them by the strictest criteria (Tosi 1975, 69–71). Adaptive behavior by organizations, then, is based on limited understanding of environmental stimuli, and on a limited view of the array of alternatives. A study of adaptive strategies, then, must consider the (limited) perspective of decision makers in given situations, and must allow for the possibility of organizational behavior which may seem irrational or self-destructive.

James D. Thompson's *Organizations in Action* takes a major step toward the integration of several theoretical perspectives on organizations, including the theories of Parsons, Selznick, March and Simon, and others. Thompson accepts both the open- and closed-systems perspectives, and uses Parsons' three levels of responsibility and control to bridge the difference between them. The technical level, he argues, is subject to criteria of rationality and operates from a closed systems perspective, whereas the institutional level is faced with more uncertainty and must rely on an open systems perspective (Thompson 1967, 10).

In order to survive, he argues, organizations seek to maintain independence from contingencies and constraints presented by the external environment, and he postulated numerous ways in which organizations do this (e.g., buffering, smoothing, forecasting, rationing, cooptation, cooperation, contracting). Three major concepts from his book that bear directly on this research include: task environment, organizational domain, and boundary spanning.

Task environment refers to those parts of an organization's environment that bear directly on goal setting and attainment, a subset of the total external environment (Thompson 1967, 27–28, 72). Task environments vary along such factors as degree of stability, homogeneity, or organizational density. These variables have direct bearing on the constraints felt by organizations and, therefore, on adaptive strategies.

Complex organizations operate in a maze of dependency-power relationships with other organizations and elements of the task environment. What the organization controls is considered its domain and what it does not control it must obtain from its environment. In another sense, domain refers to what the organization stakes out as its purpose or function (clients, technology, values). Thompson adopts the Parsonian perspective on organizational power as the ability to solve dependency problems. He argues that organizations will use a variety of strategies to obtain power such as cooptation (from Selznick 1949), formal contracting, and cooperation (Thompson 1967, 25–29).

Boundary spanning in Thompson's work refers to organizational mechanisms for adjusting to other organizations in the task environment not under the control of the focal organization. Boundary spanning activities vary according to the degree of heterogeneity in the task environment, and may include surveillance of activities in the environment, bargaining with actors in the environment, or forecasting and research. Organizations address the contingencies presented by their task environments through boundary spanning activities. This is an important concept for the study of organizational adaptation, because survival and inter-organizational power issues tend to be played out at the boundaries or intersecting points of organizations (Thompson 1967, 70–73).

Jeffrey Pfeffer's review of different perspectives in formal organization theory also provides valuable insights for this research. Resource dependency theory attempts to integrate the external control and rational action approaches to the study of organizations, by viewing organizational behavior as an emergent process. Recognizing that organizations are influenced by their environments, Pfeffer argues that at the same time they seek to manage their environments, or at least provide the illusion of control for organizational members and significant others (Pfeffer 1982, 192–202). Organizational behavior emerges as the result of interplay between internal and external forces. This perspective allows the researcher to consider multiple sources of organizational behavior without abandoning any of the major sociological perspectives on action. Pfeffer explains that it is up to the student of organizational behavior to select the proper methods and models to research organizations, and to allow for multiple levels of analysis (Pfeffer 1982, 10–14).

Pfeffer and Salancik discuss a number of significant issues for this research in *The External Control of Organizations* (1978). They present the resource dependency perspective on organizations in a detailed and comprehensive manner. Three concepts they define as critical to the "contextual" perspective on organizations include:

1. Organizational Effectiveness—Pfeffer and Salancik define organizational effectiveness as "...the ability to create acceptable outcomes and actions...an external standard of how well an organization is meeting the demands of groups and organizations concerned with its activities." Organizational acceptability, they argue, is ultimately dependent on outsiders, and organizations attempt to manipulate outside factors to create acceptability (Pfeffer and Salancik 1978, 11).

2. Organizational Environment—they accept the vagueness of this concept, since not all environmental factors are felt by organizations, and not all of them are important. Buffering and loose coupling act to provide safety devices, or slack, for organizations. In addition, organizational environment is the perceived environment, based on selective gathering and analysis of information about the environment (Pfeffer and Salancik 1978, 13).

3. Organizational Constraints—these are environmental influences that produce non-random, or predictable, organizational responses. They are often considered undesirable, but Pfeffer and Salancik point out that organizations cannot survive without constraints. They maintain that environmental constraints on organizations explain why individuals in organizations account for little of the observed variation in organizational activity (Pfeffer and Salancik 1978, 14–15).

Pfeffer and Salancik do not ignore the possibility of individually motivated action in organizations—the rational perspective. They integrate external and internal perspectives on organizational action in the same way that Thompson (1967) does through the role of organizational managers. Pfeffer and Salancik argue that managers perform three important functions in organizations: symbolic figures, organizers of support and resources, and recognition of constraints and choosing organizational adjustments (Pfeffer and Salancik 1978, 17–18).

With these concepts as their starting point, Pfeffer and Salancik review a broad range of organizational issues and organization-environment interactions, with a focus on adaptability and survival. For the purposes of this research, their discussion of how organizations manage external demands is worth reviewing. Unless organizations comply fully with demands placed on them, a losing proposition, they can adapt to or avoid external influences or dependence on resources in a variety of ways. These include, but are not limited to, selective or sequential attention to conflicting demands, attempts to manipulate the environment by controlling demand or controlling the definition of satisfaction, secrecy or information control, diversification or merger, cooptation, or buffering (Pfeffer and Salancik 1978, 94–109).

Bidwell and Kasarda critique resource dependency, or contingency, theory in *The Organization and Its Ecosystem* (1985). Theoretical developments in organization theory from Weber to Parsons to March and Simon to Perrow to Pfeffer and Salancik, they argue, actually fall short of true open system theory because they do not explain how organizations change. According to them, organization theories have moved from "closed" to "control system" theories by addressing organizational environment as an influence on organizational structure, and by explaining why organizations, or organization types, differ. They have yet to account for the emergence of organizational structure (Bidwell and Kasarda 1985, 21–23). Bidwell and Kasarda advance the ecological approach to organizations found in Aldrich (1979), Hannan and Freeman (1977), and others, as the following quote demonstrates:

> ...we assume that the constraints of the collectivity level systems on individual behavior are sufficiently strong to allow the exclusion of micro-social events from an explanation of the activity of the system...These system constraints allow one to treat aggregative properties of the organizational collectivity as among its unit properties and to trace their reciprocal relationships without appeal to the mediation of interpersonal ties or exchanges. (Bidwell and Kasarda 1985, 25)

Bidwell and Kasarda assume that organizations and environments are part of an ecosystem that includes technological and other resources, organization structure and activities, the relationships between organization and environment activities, and the number and kinds of people who perform them. Viewing organizations in this manner moves organization theory toward a more dynamic and explanatory (and sociological) realm (Bidwell and Kasarda 1985, 23–26).

Pfeffer anticipated Bidwell and Kasarda's argument in *Organizations and Organization Theory* (1982). He compares resource dependency theory to population ecology theory and finds them comparable in one respect. Both are concerned with emergent phenomena — resource dependency theory with emergent behavior, population ecology theory with emergent organizational forms. Pfeffer notes the following as differences between the two perspectives:

1. Level of analysis—population ecology is concerned with populations of organizations, whereas resource dependency is concerned with individual organizations.

2. Time frame—population ecology has a longer, evolutionary perspective.

3. Environment—resource dependency sees environment as in a more reciprocal relationship with organizations than does population ecology (though Bidwell and Kasarda would debate this).

4. Life cycle—population ecology is more concerned with the birth and death processes of organizations or organizational forms, whereas resource dependency is concerned with adaptive behavior.

5. Rationality—resource dependency assumes more rationality in organizations than population ecology, which recognizes variation and selection processes (Pfeffer 1982, 204–205).

The nature of this research, a case study in the adaptation and survival of one complex organization, concerns itself more with the resource dependency perspective than population ecology. The research problem has to do with the mechanisms by which Patuxent adapts to its environment, not with the birth, death, or emergence of treatment-oriented prisons. This study, then, relies more on the resource dependency perspective, with its links to theoretical developments from Parsons to Pfeffer (and Salancik), than on population ecology.

This review of sociological approaches to organizations provides a general perspective, and a starting point for further review of theory. Parsons' discussion of integration, power, and levels of responsibility in organizations; March and Simon's discussion of limited rationality; Thompson's view of organizations as adaptive, problem solving systems; and Pfeffer and Salancik's resource dependency perspective represent the dominant themes in the sociology of organizations with relevance to the study of Patuxent Institution. From a different perspective, it is through an in-depth case study of a single organization like Patuxent Institution that these theoretical concepts come alive for the student of organizations. How, for example, do we conceptualize integration for a prison, or levels of responsibility within a prison? How does a prison adapt to its environment, and how do we conceptualize the environment of a prison? Finally, if we accept the notion that organizational survival, or success, is linked to how organizational actors solve resource dependency problems, then how does this work for a prison?

It is important to ask these theoretical questions for prisons because rarely is the study of prisons (or public organizations in general) conducted with such a focus on organizational theory. As we apply theoretical concepts to the case of Patuxent Institution, we find that they are not always so neat and tidy. Power, for example, is both ceded and forcefully applied. Dependency on external resources is not necessarily a weakness for an organization. However, before we delve more deeply into these questions, we must explore organization theory more fully.

The Special Case of Public Organizations

Most organization theory is concerned with general organizational concepts, or is geared to private sector organizations. This research on Patuxent Institution considers the distinction between public and private (and quasi-public) organizations an important one. Definitions of public organizations tend to focus on such variables as organizational goals, structure, or environment. While a universal definition of "public organization" may be elusive, the existence of major variation along these lines between public and private organizations provides a useful focus for this research.

Peabody and Rourke define public bureaucracies as organizations that are generally part of government, employ public servants, perform activities of a public nature, are open to scrutiny, and have concern with the "public interest" (Peabody and Rourke, in March 1965, 802).

Hill (1972) cites three similar characteristics of public organizations: (1) the salience of social values in the everyday workings of public organizations, (2) the unique level of commitment from employees (less than members of voluntary organizations, and more than industrial workers), and (3) the high level of conflict surrounding public organizations.

Rainey, Backoff, and Levine (1976) present a list of differentiating characteristics of public organizations along three dimensions: environmental factors, organization-environment transactions, and internal structure and processes. These are considered below:

Environmental Factors

1. Market exposure—public organizations have less involvement with the economic market as a source of resources, information, and constraints that produce incentives for cost

reduction and efficiency. They are involved in an appropriation process which de-emphasizes efficiency.

2. Legal and formal constraints—public organizations are more constrained by laws concerning their purpose, methods, and spheres of operations than are private organizations.

3. Political influences—public organizations experience a greater diversity and intensity of influence from legislatures and interest groups. This involves them in complex bargaining processes with organizations in the task environment, and produces a greater need to build and maintain support.

Organization-Environment Transactions

1. Coerciveness—the monopolistic nature of some government organizations necessitates that extensive control mechanisms be applied to them.

2. Policy impact—public organizations have potentially greater impact on citizens due to the scope of their activities, their symbolic influence, and their closeness to political power.

3. Public scrutiny and public expectations—citizens have more right to obtain information from public organizations than they do from private ones, and they can have more influence on their activities.

4. Goods produced—public organizations typically produce services, or public goods, which are difficult to affix prices to.

Internal Structures and Processes

1. Goals—public organizations tend to have a multiplicity and diversity of objectives and evaluation criteria, which may be vague and conflicting.[3]

2. Role of the administrator—public organizations have weaker, or fragmented, hierarchical authority structures that are less flexible than those found in private organizations.

3. Dysfunctions—public organizations are sometimes characterized as over-bureaucratized ("red tape"), routinized with little innovation or incentives, and timid (Rainey, Backoff, and Levine 1976, 98–103).

Wamsley and Zald's discussion of the political economy model for the analysis of public organizations provides another important focus for this research. They argue, too, that there are valid reasons for differentiating private organizations from public organizations. While private and public organizations face similar constraints, different weights apply to major variables affecting the public organization, and the difference lies in the impact of politics. Organization leaders tend to be political figures, organization goals are less often guided by cost principles, and even the most basic economic decisions tend to become political issues. Following Wamsley and Zald, then, the key to Patuxent's survival lies in the management of its political economy, including such organization variables as legitimacy patterns, outside perceptions of agency expertise, development of key outside supporters, and the distribution of power resources in the external environment (Wamsley and Zald 1973, 1–15).

While public organizations may lack a formal definition, and though some of the definitive criteria mentioned above remain untested by empirical research, the discussion of public organizations in contrast to private ones points to other issues worthy of consideration for this research. As a formal organization, Patuxent Institution exhibits many of the characteristics listed as definitive of public organizations: conflicting goals and ambiguous evaluation criteria, close public scrutiny, imposition of legal constraints, and influence of politics on organizational operations. These elements must all be considered in the study of Patuxent's survival.

Case Studies of Organizations

This section discusses several studies on prisons and other organizations as a review of: (1) sociological contributions to the study of prisons as formal organizations (plus one book about Patuxent by a psychologist), and (2) current knowledge concerning organizational survival and adaptation. We review the well-known (among penologists) case studies of prisons by Sykes, Clemmer, Jacobs, and others, and then turn to more recent historical and theoretical treatises on corrections and punishment (e.g., Garland, and Morris and Rothman). First, however, for a more complete perspective, we examine empirical studies of the survival and adaptation of organizations other than prisons and total institutions found in Kimberly's study of rehabilitation workshops, Kaufman's study of survival among federal agencies, Bowman and Snyder's study of the Selective Service System, and Wilson's study of a Midwestern college.

Kimberly's study of sheltered workshops finds support for the assertions of Clemmer (1958), Stinchcombe (1965), and Burns (1967) that social structure influences organizational structure. Kimberly's study examines the funding sources of 123 sheltered workshops, and uses percentage of funding from production activities as a means of distinguishing between production- and rehabilitation-oriented workshops. Kimberly finds that workshops founded prior to World War II exhibit different structures (orientations, funding sources) than those founded after the war. Specifically, more post-war workshops than pre-war workshops have a rehabilitation orientation, which relates to historical trends in government funding policies (and likely to changing perspectives on the nature of mental illness and mental deficiencies, Kimberly 1975, 6–8).

Kaufman's study conducted for the Brookings Institution examines the birth, death, and longevity of federal agencies from a population ecology perspective. Kaufman studied the factors influencing the organizational life cycle for 421 federal agencies from 1923 to 1973. He found that federal agencies have great survival ability—85 percent of those in existence in 1923 were still in existence in 1973. The average birth rate of federal agencies remained fairly constant over the years, though there was a move from statutory to executive or administrative creation, reflecting the increase in the power of the presidency over those years. Longevity is not related to statutory creation, and he found that statutorily created agencies fall prey to non-statutory actions. Federal agencies exhibit a lower death rate than private businesses, and the following factors play a role in organizational deaths: poor leadership, political changeover, inability to meet new demands, dissatisfaction with organizational performance, competition, and completion of mission (Kaufman 1976, 60).

Bowman and Snyder present a descriptive account of the rise, decline, and re-emergence of the Selective Service System over a ten-year period beginning in the mid-1970s. The variables they attribute to the agency's survival include support networks and good relations with congressional committees, the statutory base, perceived importance of mission, size, and leadership and vitality (Bowman and Snyder 1985, 159–161).

Wilson describes the death of a Midwestern college, explaining the process along temporal and spatial dimensions. The temporal dimension includes historical trends such as the change from charismatic to absentee leadership; changes in the characteristics of the student population (from unorthodox to routinized to radical) and in the faculty (from an older, smaller, broadly educated faculty to a faculty of accredited specialists with disciplinary distinction); and also the organizational change from a college to a network of campuses to a university. These changes reflected centrifugal forces (outside influences) that were not counteracted by centripetal forces that would have increased commitment to the college's original goals and orientation. The spatial dimension includes such environmental influences as the economic problems of the 1970s and the decline in student enrollment, politicization of the staff; cooptation of the college by sports, media, military; "junk food" establishments and organizational susceptibility to common cultural currents, the principle of innovation or change for change's sake, and equality and pluralism to the detriment of a functional division of labor (Wilson 1985, 264–276). Wilson concluded that there is a constant interplay in an organization between purpose, procedures, and product, and that organizational leaders must monitor the interaction between these entities at all times. Changes in organizational input should tip leaders off to impacts on the organization. He cited permeability as a crucial variable in organizational survival. Finally, he concluded that, in order to survive, organizations must maintain a balance between centrifugal forces (differentiation) and centripetal forces (common commitment) (Wilson 1985, 277–278).

Prison Studies

Sociological studies of prisons conducted over the past five decades relied heavily on the open systems perspective of Parsons, Shils, Katz and Kahn, Perrow, and Thompson, and have contributed greatly to our understanding of how prisons, as social systems, interact with the larger social environment. The studies of Clemmer, Sykes, Goffman, and Jacobs demonstrate that in order to understand life in prison, one must understand prisons as sub-systems of the larger social order. This section reviews some of the major studies of prisons and considers their value for this research.

Donald Clemmer is recognized as the pioneer of the community perspective in prison research (Jacobs 1977, 2; Hood and Sparks 1970, 217). He studied the maximum-security psychiatric prison at Menard, Illinois, in the 1930s and published *The Prison Community* in 1940 (revised in 1958). Clemmer viewed Menard as a microcosm of society and noted the relationship between the prison and its local, regional, and national environments in such aspects of the prison community as: (1) the classification and stratification of inmates into "Elites," "Hoosiers," and "Middle Class" (an inmate's position in this scheme was determined in large part by the geographic region and subculture from which he came), and (2) the impact the Depression had on the types of inmates and patterns of criminality found in the prison. Clemmer noted that such influences are temporary. He did not expect them to endure over many years because changes in social conditions outside the prison (economics, politics, and values) would eventually be reflected on the inside (Jacobs 1977, 2–3).

Gresham Sykes' *The Society of Captives* (1958) echoes Clemmer's notion that prisons are open systems. His study of Trenton (New Jersey) State Prison in the mid-1950s began with an interest in the theory and practice of systems of total power (Sykes 1958, xiv–xv). Sykes concluded that the exercise of total power in a maximum-security prison is a myth, for reasons directly related to the prison's link with society. Sykes explained that prisons are more permeable than they appear for a variety of reasons. As instruments of the state, they are shaped by social and political influences, and they function in a relationship with the larger social order. As various interest groups (e.g., political, religious, ethnic, and welfare) seek to influence the goals and practices of prisons, prisons find themselves acting on or reacting to the free community. Additionally, prison personnel, who often come from the same cultures that inmates come from, work closely with inmates on a daily basis in what Sykes calls an "uneasy compromise" to get the job of running a prison done. These factors work against the authority of the totalitarian regime that is supposed to be maintained by the prison's custodial force. The political nature of prison objectives, the struggle of various outside interest groups for influence in the prison, and the necessity of maintaining an informal compromise with inmates (to maintain order within the walls) all contribute to the ineffectiveness of total power in the prison (Sykes 1958, 8).

In *Newjack* (2000), Ted Conover gives a journalistic account of his experience as a correctional officer trainee, then a prison officer, at New York's Sing Sing prison. This unique (journalistic) perspective on prison life re-affirms Sykes' discoveries about the negotiation of control between inmates and officers behind prison bars, as the following excerpt illustrates:

> ...After weeks of hanging out with senior officers who seemed to bring little more to the job than machismo and forbearance, who would say things like "If they're happy, you're not doing your job," here was a guy...who saw gallery work as an art, something you could perform creatively...Smith melded toughness with an attitude of respect for the inmates. In turn, he was respected back. What he seemed to understand was that at the root of the job was the inevitability of a kind of relationship between us and them... (Conover, 2000, 92)

James Jacobs, in *Stateville* (1977), relies on the open-systems perspective to reveal the changing nature of that prison's integration with society, which produced changes in the prison's internal authority structure. Drawing from Weber's (1947) discussion of authority and Shils' (1962) essay on mass society, Jacobs relates how Stateville transformed from an authoritarian (charismatic) regime removed from society's center in the early to mid-1900s to a rational-bureaucratic regime closer to the center in the 1970s. He provides a detailed account of how four processes (erosion of local autonomy, professionalization of administration, organizational growth, and politicization of prison issues) worked to change how Stateville related to mass society, characterized especially by the increasing ability of outside influences (law, interest groups, and federal policies) to have an impact on internal operations.

Steve Martin and Sheldon Eckland-Olson provide a similarly insightful account of the Texas prison system in *Texas Prisons: The Walls Came Tumbling Down* (1987). They relate a quarter century of struggle for reform in Texas prisons, marked by court battles and a recalcitrant and corrupt prison administration, eventually aided by an activist judge. As Jacobs described in *Stateville,* Martin and Eckland-Olson also show that it requires the intrusion of the legal system inside the prison walls, often against the stronghold of an entrenched bureaucracy and charismatic leaders (in Texas' case, George Beto), in a process that takes many years, to effect changes in America's brutal prison systems.

Francis Carney in *Criminality and Its Treatment: The Patuxent Experience* (1989) provides the only previously existing case study about Patuxent Institution.[4] Carney's focus is on the treatment of prisoners, psychopathy, and the application of psychotherapy in the prison setting, and he does not address some of the more sociological questions raised in this book. He does, however, provide some illuminating material (based on over 30 years of experience as a correctional psychologist) on the psychological aspects of prison life, treatment of addictions, and treatment of pedophilia.[5] Echoing an oft-repeated dilemma, Carney concludes that American corrections will continue to experience high recidivism rates unless the tension between treatment and punishment behind bars is reduced or resolved (Carney, 1989, p. 146).

David Garland, in *Punishment and Modern Society* (1990), performs an admirable service for those of us who recognize punishment (or "penality" as he calls it) as a complex social and cultural phenomenon, and who wish to understand punishment from multiple perspectives (e.g., historical, psychological, legal, cultural), by articulating a sociology, or theory, of punishment. Thinking of punishment as a social institution like the family, law, religion, education, or government, he argues, helps us understand punishment as a slowly evolving means for resolving social needs (such as enforcing laws, enhancing social solidarity, regulating populations, conveying values and cultural meanings, and ensuring safety). Garland notes, as well, that this institutional perspective helps us understand how prisons and punishment are linked to other social institutions, and how, when one views punishment as sets of practices, meanings, historical experiences, and normative rules, within the institution of punishment are conflicts and tensions that seem at times to be in direct opposition to each other.

Norval Morris and David Rothman provide excellent background material for this notion in *The Oxford History of the Prison* (1995). Noting the tendency to view prisons as monolithic, permanent fixtures in Western society, these authors compiled a collection of essays on the nature and function(s) of prisons from the ancient and medieval worlds, through early modern Europe, through eighteenth century prisons in England and the U.S. (and the Australian convict colonies), up the present-day "modern" prisons. They, too, note that Western societies have expectations of prisons that are "unreal and contradictory" (Morris and Rothman, 1995, xi).

Neo-institutional Theory

Walter Powell and Paul DiMaggio published a synthesis of theoretical and empirical work (dubbed "neo-institutionalism") in the field of complex organizations in *The New Institutionalism in Organizational Analysis* (1991) that provides remarkable insight to some of these observations by the penologists of our day. Their review of theoretical perspectives on organizations, organizational development, and organizational survival differs from the classical and traditional theoretical perspectives reviewed above in the following ways:

- Neo-institutional theory stresses the relationship between organizational stability and legitimacy and the power of common understandings among organization members, while traditional organization theory emphasizes vested interests as a result of tradeoffs and alliances.

- Neo-institutional theory recognizes, better than other theories, the sources of irrationality in organization structures. Traditional organization theory emphasizes a "shadowland of informal integration," to illustrate deviations from organization constraints, but does not deal as directly with irrationality as neo-institutional theory.

- Neo-institutional theory sees organization environments as subtle in their influence, as creating "lenses through which [organization] actors view the world," while traditional organization theory views organizations as embedded in local environments, tied together with communities by multiple loyalties of organization members. Loyalty is seen as negotiated via face-to-face interaction.

- Neo-institutional theory views the institutionalization process (the process by which organization forms or fields develop) as occurring at the societal level, while traditional organization theory assumes that organizations are institutionalized and, in and of themselves, provide the key loci of the institutionalization process (in other words, traditional organization theory tends to ignore organizational development). Neo-institutional theory views institutionalization as a cognitive and cultural process through which individuals organize information with the help of social categories (Powell and DiMaggio 1991, 12–15).

Neo-institutional theory is not a radical departure from traditional and classical theories; rather it is a progression, a step in organizational theory development that builds on existing work but places emphasis on areas that bring organizational theory and research more into the realm of the sociological. It places more emphasis on organization culture and the role of broader culture in the development of organization forms. There is less orientation to concepts of power, politics, and exchange and more orientation to cognitive and symbolic interaction processes. A greater role is seen for super-organizational (sectoral or societal) forces in the development and survival of organization forms.

Friedland and Alford (1991) describe the new sociological direction of neo-institutional theory as a non-functionalist conception of organizations and organizational development that must work at three levels of analysis—individual, organizational, and institutional—but without abandoning the political, exchange approach to organizations:

> It is the content of an institutional order that shapes the mechanisms by which organizations are able to conform or deviate from established patterns. These institutional orders, and the specific relations between them, delimit types of organizational fields. From an institutionalist perspective, organizations which adopt the appropriate forms perform well not because they are most efficient, but because these forms are most effective at eliciting resources from other organizations which take them to be legitimate. (Friedland and Alford 1991, 243–244)

Consider DiMaggio's (1991) case study in neo-institutional research in "Constructing an Organizational Field as a Professional Project: U.S. Art Museums, 1920–1940." He describes the development of art museums as a local phenomenon, but guided by the "emergence of fieldwide structures" at the national level, and also guided by organizing by actors who wanted to change the museum's structure and mission. For example, DiMaggio describes three contributory factors to the development of art museums:

1. Professionalization and organization by museum workers;
2. Reliance on institutional rather than technical sources of legitimacy; and

3. An appeal to concepts of professional expertise, service delivery, and disinterest in monetary gain as special characteristics of art museums (DiMaggio 1991, 286–289).

Summary of Theoretical Perspectives

The open systems perspective on organizations focuses on issues of integration (how organizations fit into their environments and society in general, and how individuals and groups fit together in organizations), power (maintenance of dominance or independence in the environment and the ability to obtain necessary resources), and organizational behavior at its boundaries (boundary spanning and limited rationality, and adaptive strategies). When we consider the special issues pertaining to public organizations in the general context of open system theory (e.g., influence of politics, non-market-driven values), the research focus for the survival and adaptive strategies of a unique prison such as Patuxent Institution becomes clearer. Patuxent, like all prisons, is an open system, as sociologists since the 1940s have demonstrated. Therefore adaptive mechanisms similar to those found in other types of organizations may be found.

As a public organization, Patuxent experiences the impacts and constraints of values, culture, and politics in many ways, perhaps more so than other organizations. The variations in adaptive behavior found at Patuxent will most likely be the result of a unique mix of managerial (individual), organizational, and institutional influences—constant concern with issues of legitimacy, dependence on outside elements for resources, susceptibility to public and political criticism, and reliance on societal and institutional myths (or cultural constructs) about corrections and rehabilitation.

Notes

1. This selection of prison studies represents a small portion of the large number of journalistic, sociological, theoretical, managerial, and other types of books, reports, and manuscripts that have been written on all types of prisons over the past 50 years. They have been selected primarily for their sociological orientation. Some (the Conover, Early, and Bergner books, in particular) are journalistic in their perspective, yet they touch on key sociological issues.

2. While somewhat dated, Parsons (1960) defined organizations as social units (or human groupings) deliberately constructed and reconstructed to seek specific goals. While Thomson (1967) addresses his work to "organizations which induce or coerce participation" (versus voluntary organizations), the simple definition offered by Parsons serves the purpose of this book. Prisons are complex organizations that both induce (from employees) and coerce (from inmates) participation; their complexity lies in their size, levels of organization and activity, multiplicity of goals, and integration with other external criminal justice and other organizations.

3. This is especially true for prisons and criminal justice organizations in general. See Garland (1990) and Morris and Rothman (1995) for contemporary discussions of this long-understood phenomenon in American corrections.

4. While written from the psychological standpoint, Carney's book covers some of the same historical and sociological ground covered here. Other reports have been written about Patuxent, most notably two research reports commissioned by the Maryland legislature during times of great controversy surrounding Patuxent (and reviewed later on in this book), and at least one

other doctoral thesis was based on Patuxent Institution (Longmire 1979). John DiIulio makes passing reference to Patuxent in his book *No Escape: The Future of American Corrections* (1991).

5. One of Carney's most interesting works (in my opinion) is his unpublished manuscript *The Will to Fail* (written in the late 1980s), in which he takes a more personal view of the treatment of criminals and its attendant frustrations for inmates and treatment providers alike.

Chapter Three

Framework for the Analysis of Patuxent Institution

This chapter draws from the literature review in the previous chapter and presents a framework for analyzing how Patuxent adapts to its environment and survives. The framework illuminates the process by which survival issues are, hypothetically, managed by the Institution, as well as the theory underlying the process. Such a framework for analysis must include: (a) grounding in experience and theory, (b) a defined structure, and (c) sufficient background and descriptive detail about the research case to make categorizations and explanations meaningful.

In presenting a framework for the analysis of Patuxent's adaptation, we review concepts and definitions from the work of Talcott Parsons and other organization environment theorists to define the structure and components of the framework. Then we describe the cases in the analysis and the data collection and analysis procedures, thus setting the stage for the presentation of findings.

Structure and Components of the Framework

The framework for the analysis of Patuxent Institution's environment interactions contains two levels of specificity—the theoretical level: the theories of Parsons and other organization theorists that provide the broad framework for the analysis, and the experiential: descriptive information about Patuxent and its environment that brings the theoretical framework to life.

Parsons describes three levels of responsibility and control in organizations. These include the institutional (the level concerned with achievement of organization goals), managerial (the level concerned with managing the technical level), and technical (the level concerned with the performance of primary organizational tasks) (Parsons 1965, 60–65, Thompson 1967, 10–11). We utilize this perspective on organizations for analysis by defining three levels of responsibility and control in Patuxent Institution and its external environment, and using that framework as the setting in which Patuxent-environment interactions take place. Table 1 presents a matrix of institution and environment levels of responsibility and control (a la Parsons)—the key framework for this analysis.

Table 1 depicts the two domains in which organizational responsibility and control are conceptualized—Patuxent and its environment, consisting of state, local, and national components. The cells in Table 1 contain the components of the framework—the matrix of organizations, actors, or coalitions that operate within the specified levels. These domains and levels are described below.

The institutional level of responsibility and control for Patuxent consists of its governing board—The Citizens Advisory Board (formerly the Board of Patuxent Institution), Patuxent's Executive Director, and the Associate Directors.

Under current law (Title 4 of the Maryland Code, Correctional Services) the Governor appoints the Citizens Advisory Board based on the recommendation of the Secretary of Public Safety and Correctional Services. The law does not prescribe the specific membership of the Board. In the past it comprised the Executive Director of Patuxent, legal professionals from Maryland (law professors and practicing lawyers), social science professionals, and citizens. It has taken several different forms since 1960, when Patuxent was granted independence from the Maryland Department of Corrections and placed under the control of the Governing Board. It serves a function similar to that of the board of directors of a corporation: it reviews organizational goals, operations, problems, trends, and sets organizational direction.

Table 1

Framework for the Analysis of Patuxent/Environment Interactions

	Environment		
Level of Responsibility and Control	**Patuxent**	**State/Local**	**National**
Institutional	• Governing Board • Executive Director • Associate Directors	• State Constitution • State Supreme Court • Legislature • Legal Culture	• U.S. Constitution • U.S. Supreme Court • Legal Culture
Managerial	• Paroling Authority • Associate Directors • Department Heads	• Public Safety Commission • Unions • Professional Associations • Courts • Press/Media • Citizen Coalitions	• U.S. Department of Justice • Professional Associations • Press/Media
Technical	• Clinical Staff • Education Staff • Correctional Staff • Medical Staff • Other Staff	• Criminal Justice System	• Criminal Justice System

The Executive Director is the chief executive of Patuxent. This position oversees treatment (clinical) as well as the other traditional operations of prisons (educational and vocational programs, custody, maintenance, personnel, budget, planning, medical, and so on). Administratively, the Executive Director answers to the Secretary of Public Safety and Correctional Services.[1]

Currently, Patuxent has two associate directors, one for Behavioral Sciences and one for Psychiatry, and another senior administrator, the Warden. These three positions at Patuxent are responsible for administration, treatment, and custody, respectively. The law establishes their positions, as well as the Executive Director position, and all three work closely with the Executive Director in the establishment of goals for their areas as well as for the Institution as a whole.

The Managerial level of Patuxent Institution includes the paroling authority—the Board of Review consisting of four Patuxent Administrators (the Director, two Associate Directors, and the Warden) and five community members appointed by the Governor, one of which must be a representative of a victims' rights association. The Board of Review's composition and operations are governed by Section 4-205 of the Annotated Code of Maryland. The Board of Review reviews the progress of inmates at Patuxent and grants or denies leave, work release, or parole status for inmates, with some of its release decisions subject to review by the Secretary of Public Safety and Correctional Services. The Associate Directors and the Warden, while performing institution-level functions as described above, act also as middle managers in the Patuxent hierarchy. They manage distinct components of Institution operations and are responsible for from approximately 20 to over 250 personnel (as in the case of the Warden, who manages the entire custodial force).

The Executive Director designates the department heads at Patuxent, though formal approval comes from the state Department of Public Safety and Correctional Services. At the time of this writing, there were department heads for administration, finance and personnel, research, psychology, psychiatry, security, community services, and several other special program areas.[2] The managers of each of several treatment units, who supervised up to 10 staff each, are also counted as department heads, though they provide direct clinical services on a regular basis in addition to their administrative duties.

The remainder of the Patuxent staff comprises the Technical level of responsibility and control. Numbering close to 400 (including over 250 correctional officers), they perform day-to-day service delivery at Patuxent. This includes clinical services (therapy, counseling, diagnostic work, provision of social work services), medical services, correctional services, maintenance, personnel, clerical, and educational services. Appendix C presents the Fiscal Year 2002 version of the Patuxent Institution organization chart.[3]

Patuxent's Environment

Levels of responsibility and control in Patuxent's environment are less easily defined since this involves applying individual organization concepts at the societal level. There are many aspects and levels to the environment of Patuxent Institution, ranging from the local community in which it exists to the national "community" and sectors of it generally concerned with criminal justice and offender treatment issues. For our purposes, two levels of Patuxent's environment are described: the state/local level and the national level, including significant actors and groups at each level.

The national institutional environment consists of those bodies and institutions that represent federal law or the national legal culture. These include primarily the U.S. Constitution, more specifically its interpretation by the U.S. Supreme Court in cases involving Patuxent. The national legal culture is difficult to define, but can be thought of as general thinking regarding law, justice, legal ethics, criminal justice, and the goals of the legal system, as embodied in oral and written sources (e.g., educational materials, popular culture or public opinion, legal treatises).

The state institutional environment consists of similar phenomena generally found within the state of Maryland (or the surrounding metropolitan area including the District of Columbia) such as the State Constitution and its interpretation by state courts, the Maryland Legislature, and state or regional legal culture.

The national managerial environment consists of those organizations and institutions concerned with the management of criminal justice, or with the professionalization of criminal justice workers. It, too, has state counterparts. The U.S. Department of Justice, for example, contains several subunits whose function it is to foster improved criminal justice research and management at state and local levels, and to promote professionalism. These subunits fall under the Office of Justice Programs within the U.S. Department of Justice, and include such agencies as the National Institute of Justice, the National Institute of Corrections, the Bureau of Justice Assistance, and the Bureau of Justice Statistics.[4] Other professional organizations with criminal justice concerns include the American Academy of Psychiatry and the Law, the American Correctional Association, the American Psychological Association, the Correctional Education Association, and the American Association of Correctional Psychologists. In many ways, these organizations concern themselves with the administration of justice, or with treatment in criminal justice settings, by sponsoring research and grant programs (with federal or private funds), training programs and seminars in related topics, or even accreditation (for organizations) or continuing education (for professionals).

The managerial environment at the state level includes the Maryland Department of Public Safety and Correctional Services, the state agency (called a Secretariat in Maryland) under which Patuxent Institution falls along with the Maryland State Police, the Maryland Division of Correction, the Maryland Division of Parole and Probation, the Maryland Department of Mental Health, and other criminal justice and public safety agencies. The external managerial environment also includes the state employees' and correctional officers' labor unions, state level professional associations, local chapters of national professional associations, and state or local citizens' coalitions. State courts and the judiciary are included at the managerial level because, though they influence institutional goals and goal achievement, they are concerned mainly with interpretation of actions in the legal context rather than with defining Patuxent's purpose and direction. Judges, acting in their professional capacity, serve a similar function.[5]

The state-level managerial environment of Patuxent also includes the press and media. These institutions, to the extent that they reflect the general public or professional attitudes and agenda, mediate between the institutional and managerial or technical levels as conveyers of information. They may, of course, influence attitudes to such an extent that they take on an institutional function at the national and state levels.

This study considers the state and national criminal justice systems in general as the technical environment with which Patuxent Institution interacts. In reality, they are a loosely connected set of subsystems. To the extent that technical practices in the criminal justice system (e.g., security measures, personnel practices, inmate processing, and delivery of services) influence in any way the practices at Patuxent, an institution-environment interaction may occur at this level. In most cases, however, such exchanges take place in the managerial or professional association setting.

By identifying the various sources and levels of responsibility and control for Patuxent Institution (as depicted in Table 1 and described above), we present a structure for the analysis of organization-environment interactions that take place in conflict or survival-threatening situations. Utilizing Parsons' three levels of responsibility and control in complex organizations (the theoretical framework), and identifying actors, agencies, or coalitions that operate at each level (the experiential components of the framework), we posses a theoretical framework for studying the survival and adaptation of Patuxent Institution. We address three additional points regarding this analytical framework before continuing: ideal versus actual typology, interactions within and between levels, and direct and indirect influences or constraints.

Ideal Versus Actual Typology

The framework depicted here suggests that the boundaries between levels are closed and that there are clear-cut differences between the institutional, managerial, and technical levels in organizations. This is not the case in reality. The blurring of distinctions between levels is best described in the case of Patuxent Institution, for it is a relatively small organization (in comparison to the State of Maryland or the United States) and bureaucratic divisions are less distinct than in larger social structures. Consider the three Associate Directors. On any given day they may act with institutional responsibility and control (for example, when they meet with the Director of Patuxent to decide on future treatment directions), and with managerial responsibility and control (for example, when they meet with their staffs to assess workloads and develop work schedules). When the Associate Directors act in an institutional capacity, and the extent to which they do so, depends on the issue at hand and the context in which they act.[6] Similarly, department heads at Patuxent may act as managers (when they convene their departments for weekly or monthly meetings) or technicians (service deliverers, when they perform direct client-oriented services). In the sphere of Patuxent's external environment, judges may exert institution level control through their influence on society, or managerial control when they sit at the bench and perform their legal duties.

While individual roles may vary from level to level depending on context, the distinction between levels of control and responsibility is instructive as a typology and as a framework for analysis. They provide ideal typical categories in the Weberian sense—guideposts or models that actual observations can be compared against during analysis.

Interaction Within and Between Levels

Interactions that take place between Patuxent and its environment, like the roles played at different levels, are not bound within levels. Individuals or groups at Patuxent's institutional level do not interact solely with their environment's institutional level; and managers and technicians at Patuxent do not interact solely with their state or national counterparts. For example, the institutional level at Patuxent may respond to pressure from the general legal culture (say, public opinion). The managerial level at Patuxent may also respond to pressure from the general legal culture with no directives or instruction from the institutional level. Consider the decisions of the paroling authority. During the middle to late 1980s it became more restrictive in its granting of full parole to inmates—the number of paroles granted dropped from over 20 per year to a range of 10–15 per year. While no directives regarding parole came from any source, the Patuxent Director, Associate Director, other Board of Review members, and some treatment staff responded during those years to what they felt was pressure from the general legal culture to be more restrictive. An environmental constraint was felt at different levels of the organization, and it had an impact on members' behaviors.

Similarly, the technical level at Patuxent may respond to pressure or direction from any of the three environment organization levels. Officers may react to union politics or directives, to their perceptions of public opinion, or based on their understanding of what their counterparts do in other prisons, and the same may hold true for clinicians or teachers at Patuxent. Interactions between Patuxent and its environment, then, are expected to cross organizational levels.

Direct and Indirect Influences

In most instances, Patuxent will interact directly with its immediate environment—the State of Maryland, or components of its criminal justice system. For example, Patuxent may have direct exchanges with its oversight agency, the Maryland Department of Public Safety and Correctional Services, or with the Maryland legislature. In some instances these direct exchanges will be pure; that is, the conflict or interaction will have been initiated at the Patuxent-state level (as in a dispute over budgeting, allocation of staff overtime, or capital projects). In other instances, the interaction with state representatives will be an arena for an indirect Patuxent-national exchange. This would occur, for example, when state representatives follow a national trend (e.g., experimenting with different treatment modalities for sex offenders) and Patuxent reacts to the state-level initiative. In another example, the Maryland chapter of a national professional association (e.g., the American Academy of Psychiatry and the Law) may be an active chapter, and may attempt to influence treatment issues at Patuxent.

As noted above, Table 1 above provides the framework for the analysis of Patuxent Institution with the components of its environment most relevant to its mission (in Thompson's words, its "task environment"). It outlines both the general framework within which institution-organization interactions take place and the organizational components from Patuxent and its environment that are relevant to the treatment issue. The next sections in this chapter describe the "cases" for the analysis—the major threats to Patuxent's treatment goal over the years, the major actors, and the data analysis methods used to discover institution-environment dynamics.

Cases in the Analysis

This research examines three significant challenges to Patuxent Institution's treatment goal over the years. These constitute direct threats to Patuxent's treatment goal, that is, events in the task environment, and subsequent institution-environment interactions that threatened either the existence of the institution or its ability to provide treatment services to inmates. The three challenges include:

1. The controversy that surrounded the Institution in the mid- to late 1970s, and that resulted in the repeal of the Defective Delinquent statute and enactment of the Eligible Person statute. This legal change abolished the indeterminate sentence at Patuxent.

2. The prison crowding crisis in Maryland in the early 1980s, and the threat of extensive double-celling at Patuxent.

3. A subsequent controversy in the late 1980s and early 1990s surrounding release and parole practices at Patuxent, the result of which was another revision of Article 31-B.

To be sure, Patuxent has faced other threats and crises in its 50-year history. Some have been more internal in nature and less severe—for example, when staff management problems disrupt treatment practices, and others have come from Patuxent's task environment. The three selected for analysis are the most severe and salient, and cover a wide range of issues.

Major Actors

This section provides more detail about major actors by identifying persons, groups, and coalitions within and surrounding Patuxent for which data for this research were obtained.

Patuxent Institution

The major actors and groups at Patuxent for which data were obtained include the following:

- Directors,
- Associate Directors,
- department heads,
- correctional staff,
- clinical staff,
- Patuxent inmates, and
- members of the Board of Patuxent Institution (and the Citizens Advisory Board), including the Board of Review (Patuxent's paroling authority).

These represent the persons within the Institution most concerned with the direction and maintenance of the treatment goal, and with whom most institution-environment interactions take place. With almost no exceptions (except perhaps some correctional staff) these actors support the treatment goal and take some action when it is threatened.[7]

Maryland State Government and Politics

The significant actors and coalitions that come into play at the state level regarding Patuxent-environment interactions over the treatment goal include the following:

- members of the Maryland legislature, either individually or in their capacities as members of influential committees (judiciary, budget, public safety),

- members of the judicial system at the state or county level,

- state government employees and agencies outside of Patuxent, specifically the Maryland Department of Public Safety and Correctional Services and its included agencies—Maryland State Police, Maryland Division of Correction, Maryland Department of Parole and Probation, Maryland Parole Commission, Maryland Victims Compensation Board,

- the local or regional press (specifically, Baltimore and Washington, D.C. newspapers),

- citizens' coalitions in Maryland, including victims' rights groups and groups organized specifically to support or oppose Patuxent, and

- professional associations of officers, administrators, and clinical staff.

The National Environment

Significant actors in the national environment that have come into play in Patuxent-environment interactions include:

- The U.S. Supreme Court,

- individuals recognized as "national experts" in corrections or behavioral sciences (e.g., Norval Morris, Karl Menninger, Manfred Guttmacher),

- U.S. Department of Justice agencies and employees (e.g., the National Institute of Justice, the National Institute of Corrections),

- national professional associations, and

- the press and media (e.g., network news programs such as "60 Minutes," "National Public Radio," and "20/20").

In order to understand the historical development of Patuxent Institution in a sociological sense we must analyze the organization at multiple levels — the technical, managerial, and institutional. Only then can we observe and understand the different influences on Patuxent's development and adaptation. Drawing from organizational theory and research, this chapter defined and described these different levels as they relate to Patuxent Institution and its organizational environment, giving specific examples of each. In addition, we present three specific examples of bona fide threats to Patuxent's legitimacy and survival as cases in the analysis.

The review of historical information about Patuxent Institution, and the author's experience as an employee of Patuxent, revealed the above-mentioned persons, groups, and organizations as the significant actors in Patuxent-environment interactions regarding the identified threats to Patuxent's treatment goal. The data analysis process determined how the various actors, groups, or organizations were involved in each of the crises—the roles played, the dominant forces, actions taken and reactions—and the outcome of the organization-environment interaction process.

The next several chapters constitute the presentation and analysis of historical data pertaining to Patuxent Institution and the three legitimacy crises mentioned above. Following a historical view of the creation and development of Patuxent in its early years (1950 to 1960), we move in a more turbulent time in Patuxent's history (the mid-1970s through the early 1990s), and it is during these years that the key legitimacy crises that provided the cases for this analysis occurred. Thus, as we relate the history of Patuxent, we discuss and analyze its key legitimacy crises.

Notes

1. The Commissioner of Corrections in Maryland, who oversees 14 correctional institutions and over 15,000 prisoners, also reports to the Secretary of Public Safety and Correctional Services. This administrative structure, then, places the Executive Director of Patuxent in a powerful position relative to the responsibilities of the job.

2. There is no official designation of "department head," at Patuxent. The author uses the distinction to identify positions below the Associate Director level, but managerial and supervisory in nature, which are responsible for management duties—for example, planning, monitoring, staff development, and coordination. Special programs include the youth program, correctional mental health center, and other distinct areas of operation.

3. This is the most recent copy available from the Institution's Annual Reports. It is an accurate reflection of the current staffing and organization of Institution personnel.

4. Since the original research for this book was conducted, the Office of Victims Assistance was created within the Office of Justice Programs, which would count as a national entity concerned with issues relating to Patuxent.

5. They may, however, influence the direction the Institution takes indirectly through professional contacts and networks.

6. The extent to which middle managers at Patuxent (or in any other organization) act in an institutional capacity also depends on their personalities and management styles.

7. In his interviews with correctional staff, the author did not encounter anti-treatment feelings or statements.

Chapter Four

Creation of Patuxent Institution and the Early Years: 1955–1959

This chapter provides a historical review of Patuxent Institution with particular attention to the dominant persons, groups, ideas, and events that shaped the creation of Patuxent Institution and the early course of its development. It also describes the early administrative structure, operations, and local influences on Patuxent (Appendix A provides a timeline for Patuxent Institution). This review supplies the background necessary for the subsequent discussion of research findings pertaining to Patuxent's adaptation and survival.

Three primary sources provide much of the information presented here: (1) existing historical documentation from Patuxent Institution, the Maryland Department of Public Safety and Correctional Services, and various libraries in Maryland, (2) the doctoral dissertation of Dennis R. Longmire, former student at the University of Maryland Institute of Criminal Justice and Criminology, entitled, *"An Empirical Evaluation of a Treatment Program for Habitual Criminal Offenders: The Case of Patuxent Institution,"* and (3) *The Will to Fail,* the unpublished manuscript of Dr. Francis L. Carney, Chief Psychologist at Patuxent Institution from 1984 to 1989 and a practicing clinician at Patuxent for over 20 years. These two authors paid particular attention to historical detail in their own analyses of Patuxent, which helped determine the chronology of events and the linking of events in Patuxent's development to events in other local, state or national arenas. Interviews with past Patuxent employees and board members provided additional details, which helped balance and interpret information obtained from written sources.

Beginnings

Most of the documented history on Patuxent Institution begins with the murder of a milkman named John W. Anderson in 1931, an event which prompted legislative activity concerning the problem of criminals who were then called mental defectives and the eventual enactment of Maryland's "defective delinquent" law in 1951. Mention must first be made of events that took place almost a century earlier in England, somewhat later in Maryland, and nationally as well to place the creation of Patuxent in a historical socio-legal context.

In 1843, English Common Law established the M'Naghten Rule. The English court acquitted Daniel M'Naghten on the basis of insanity following his attempt to assassinate Prime Minister Sir Robert Peel. From then on, knowing the difference between right and wrong, and appreciating the consequences of one's actions—the M'Naghten Standard—was the legal test for sanity.[1] Clinical diagnoses of the "psychopathic personality disorder" (the clinical precursor to the "sociopathic" and "antisocial" personality disorders in the Diagnostic and Statistical Manual of the American Psychiatric Association) were not held to constitute legal insanity. *Spencer v. State* applied the M'Naghten Rule to Maryland in 1888 (Smith 1978). *Spencer* broadened the definition of legal insanity slightly beyond the English rule, but not enough to encompass psychopathy. A similar broadening took place in *Durham v. United States* in Washington, DC, in 1954.[2] The M'Naghten Standard and *Spencer* established the legal basis for the insanity defense in Maryland. This standard operated for approximately 50 years and was in effect for, and often mentioned in, the Duker case.[3]

At the national level, according to the prevailing doctrine in the legal and medical professions, the fields of psychiatry and psychology were held in esteem. Positivist thinking predominated (though it was soon to be on the decline), as evidenced by the following excerpts From Research Report No. 29 by the Maryland Legislative Council in a section titled, "Opinion of Leading Maryland Psychiatrists and Psychologists":

> We believe that we have reached the stage of development where the psychological and psychiatric examination of such an offender, together with his record of anti-social behavior, is justification for making recommendations for use of the indeterminate sentence, which may result in confinement for life...
>
> There is the strong probability that some such individuals should have permanent custodial care, while others may be sufficiently rehabilitated to be safely released...
>
> The problem is more important and more difficult with those criminals who have deficient emotional balance and control—the so-called psychopaths...Examination and observation by competent and experienced psychiatrists, together with recently devised projective psychological tests, is able to separate these offenders from the rest of the criminal group.
>
> Many of these individuals cannot be cured by our present treatment techniques. However, with individual and group therapy a considerable number will be able to be released safely in the community under prolonged supervision. Furthermore, there is a tendency for this condition to improve as middle life is reached." (Reiblich and Hubbard 1950, 26–27)

Dr. Manfred Guttmacher, one of Maryland's leading psychiatrists at the time and a key influential person in the creation of Patuxent, authored this section along with five other prominent physicians with state or national reputations.

Looking further back in time, Karl Menninger wrote the following in his 1926 address to the Criminal Law Section of the American Bar Association:

> ...the different group, the misbehaved group, is made up of persons acting according to the psychological, biological, chemical, and physical laws which science has to a certain degree ferreted out or correlated and summed up in such a way that we can now make some definite prophecies as to what is going to happen. In the second place, we not only know what is going to happen but we know within limits whether if a certain measure is instituted it is going to change what is otherwise going to happen.

Dr. Menninger also stated in 1930: "The only permanent solution (to the crime problem) lies in the adoption of scientific methods of dealing with crime" (Menninger 1930). In 1958, following the creation of Patuxent, Dr. Menninger made the following statement at the Annual Meeting of the American Bar Association:

> If we were to follow scientific methods, following the verdict of guilty, the offender would be detained indefinitely pending a decision as to whether or how to reintroduce him successfully into the society with which he has come into conflict. He would be painstakingly and thoroughly examined, with all the skill and knowledge of modern behavioral science, regarding his personality, assets, his liabilities, and his potentialities. The nature of the environment from which he came and its effects upon him and his effects on it likewise constitute a part of such an examination.
>
> Having arrived at some diagnostic grasp of the nature of the personality of the offender, those in charge can decide whether there is a chance that he can be redirected into an adaptation to the world he will live in...the most suitable techniques in education, industrial training, group administration, and psychotherapy should be selectively applied...If, in due time, perceptible change occurs in the subject, if he responds to the program, the process should be expedited as much as possible by finding a suitable spot in society and industry for him, and getting him out of prison control (with parole control) as quickly as possible...But some patients do not respond to our efforts, and they have to remain in the hospital, or return to it promptly after a trial home visit. And if the prisoner, like some of our psychiatric patients, cannot be changed by genuine efforts to rehabilitate him, we must look our failure in the face, and provide for his indefinitely continued confinement, regardless of the technical reasons for his assignment to us. This we owe society for its protection. (Menninger 1959)

Dr. Menninger was not alone in his espousal of psychiatric positivism and the medical model for treating habitual criminals. Grob (1985), Mahrer and Pearson (1971), Ellenberger (1970), Bromberg (1982), and Cullen and Gilbert (1982) all reviewed the history of development in psychiatry and, in the case of Cullen and Gilbert, correctional philosophy. This literature abounds with references to positivist philosophy on the parts of such eminent American psychiatrists as William Alonson White, the Gluecks, Harry Stack Sullivan, and Jerome Frank. Links are also evident between the positive philosophies in psychiatry, social work, sociology, and social psychology through the works of George Herbert Mead (1918) and W.I. Thomas (1927).

Patuxent's creation in 1950, then, came on the heels of several decades of positivist thinking in the social and behavioral sciences. It will be shown below that Patuxent's creation came about just as the positivist movement in penology was on the brink of a decline that continues to this day. It is true, though, that currents in national thinking favored the development of the medical model approach to correctional treatment. Research Report No. 29 states that in 1950, 17 other states had defective delinquent statutes, as did the District of Columbia and the federal courts (Reiblich and Hubbard 1950, 10). It was a cogent argument in 1950 that curable criminals could be distinguished from incurable ones, tested, treated, and safely released to the community.

The Duker Murder Case

Now we return to the murder case. The shooting murder of Baltimore milkman John W. Anderson by Herbert Webb Duker in 1931 sparked a series of actions (albeit a slow and sporadic series) that eventually led to the drafting and passing of Patuxent's enabling legislation: Article 31-B of the Public General Laws of Maryland. Duker pled guilty to the shooting of Anderson, and it was during his sentencing hearing in the court of Judge Joseph N. Ulman (Baltimore City) that the seed was planted for the eventual emergence of Patuxent Institution.

Judge Ulman sentenced Duker to death by hanging in October 1931.[4] In his opinion for the case Judge Ulman made two key arguments:

1. Duker, 22 years old at the time of his death sentence, had been diagnosed as a "psychopathic personality" by numerous psychiatrists, independently, at juvenile and adult correctional

centers in Maryland and New York. He was not believed to be mentally retarded or inferior. Furthermore, this diagnosis was agreed upon and testified to by psychiatrists for the State and the defendant in Judge Ulman's courtroom.

2. At the time of Duker's sentencing there was no place in Maryland to treat such criminals (those legally sane by standards set by *M'Naghten* and *Spencer*, but mentally ill by accepted medical standards). Had there been such a place, Ulman argued, Duker would have been diagnosed and treated or confined earlier and would not likely have been at liberty to murder Anderson.

Judge Ulman lamented the lack of such an institution, citing also that: (a) without a death sentence Duker would eventually go free, and (b) he would remain dangerous in or out of prison until treated (Ulman 1931). Thus, Ulman gave Duker the death sentence, which was commuted to life by Governor Albert C. Ritchie within a year.

The Duker case set the stage for the discussions and developments that led to the creation of Patuxent Institution, though Article 31-B was not to become law for over 20 years. A defective delinquent bill had actually been introduced in the Maryland legislature in 1929 (prior to the Duker case),[5] but Governor Ritchie vetoed it (Carney 1985, 2). Certainly the Great Depression and World War II were events that introduced significant diversions from these issues,[6] but there must have been other reasons for the lag in time between the Duker case and the creation of Patuxent.[7]

In addition, Research Report No. 29 of the Maryland Legislative Council, which contains the original proposed draft legislation for Article 31-B, mentions two other heinous crimes that caught the attention of the Maryland public and criminal justice system around the time of Duker's case. One concerned the case of a man named Eugene James, a sex offender who brutally murdered a young girl in Baltimore. An indeterminate sentence for defective delinquents, some felt, would have prevented James from being at liberty (after a history of short sentences for sex crimes) and having the opportunity to murder. Reference is also made in that report to the Salinger case (1950), in which a jury found Salinger (a chronic violent offender and, according to Dr. Manfred Guttmacher, a "defendant [who] has no real moral judgement...is certain to become engaged in very serious criminal activities in the future") to be legally insane so that he would receive an indeterminate sentence to the state hospital for the criminally insane, rather than receive another determinate sentence, which would ensure an earlier release (Reiblich and Hubbard 1950, 4–7).

Manfred Guttmacher, perhaps the most influential physician involved in the creation of Patuxent, was the Chief Medical Officer of the Medical Services of the Supreme Bench of Baltimore at the time of Duker's arrest and trial. He conducted the psychiatric evaluation of Duker for the Court. He also conducted Salinger's evaluation. Dr. Guttmacher helped recruit Patuxent's first Director and served as an advisor and board member in Patuxent's early years.

Interest in Ulman's ideas took hold again in 1947. In that year the Maryland legislature adopted Joint Resolution 16 authorizing the creation of the Commission to Study Medico-Legal Psychiatry, with 15 members appointed by Governor William P. Lane, Jr. The Committee members included psychiatrists, other physicians, legislators, citizens, and penologists. The Commission was to examine the possibility of providing institutions and facilities for the care and treatment of criminals with mental disorders, through "...an intelligent correlation between the law and modern psychiatry" (Reiblich and Hubbard 1950, 8).

The Committee presented its report to Governor Lane and the Maryland General Assembly in December 1948. The report contained 15 recommendations that became the foundation of Patuxent Institution, summarized below:

- Creation of a Medical Court Service for pre- and post-trial psychiatric examinations, with a staff of psychiatrists and psychologists;

- Legal procedures for the determination of defective delinquency;

- Indeterminate confinement for defective delinquents;

- A new institution for defective delinquents; and

- A Board of Review to determine the suitability of defective delinquents for release to the community, yearly re-examination while in confinement, and release procedures.

It is significant to note that Duker's parole hearing took place during the Committee's work and contributed to a resurgence of discussion about treatment of such criminals.

At the same time that the Commission to Study Medico-Legal Psychiatry was deliberating, the Maryland Board of Corrections appointed an Advisory Board of seven psychologists and psychiatrists to study the problem of mentally defective inmates. The Advisory Board submitted its report in January 1949. There was some controversy between the reports of the Commission and the Advisory Board, which led to public hearings and discussion by legislators. A meeting was called between the two groups to discuss their differences, and a memorandum of agreement emerged from this meeting in May 1949. The memorandum contained essentially the same points in the Commission's report, with additional details concerning location of the new institution for defective delinquents, construction, and staff. The new institution was to be located in Jessup, Maryland (the current site of Patuxent), on State land that had already been earmarked for prison construction.

The Legislative Council of Maryland appointed the Committee on Medico-Legal Procedure in September 1949 to consider all of these developments and draft legislation to implement the new institution for defective delinquents. In this Committee's report, the following were cited as the historical developments leading up to its task at hand:

1. increase in crime,

2. the Duker case and other "horrible murders,"[8] and

3. criticism of criminal justice procedures in Maryland by medical authorities (Reiblich and Hubbard 1950, 7).

Patuxent Institution Opens for Defective Delinquents

The Maryland legislature passed Article 31-B in 1951 and appropriated money for construction of the new facility, Patuxent Institution.[9] When Patuxent Institution opened its doors in January 1955, Article 31-B defined a defective delinquent as:

> ...an individual who, by the demonstration of persistent aggravated antisocial or criminal behavior, evidences a propensity toward criminal activity, and who is found to have either such intellectual deficiency or emotional unbalance, or both, as to clearly demonstrate an actual danger to society.

Only offenders convicted and sentenced in Maryland could be recommended for examination at Patuxent for defective delinquency. One of the following five conditions had to be met before someone could request for an examination at Patuxent. The offender had to be convicted and sentenced for:

1. a felony,

2. a misdemeanor punishable by imprisonment in the penitentiary,

3. a violent crime,

4. a sex crime involving physical force or violence, disparity of age between an adult and a minor, or a sexual act of an uncontrolled or repetitive nature, or

5. two or more offenses punishable by imprisonment in a criminal court of the state. (Reiblich and Hubbard 1950, 31).

Procedures and Operations

Procedurally, a state's attorney, the Chairman of the Board of Corrections, or the defendant's attorney could refer an offender to Patuxent for evaluation as a defective delinquent,[10] after a conviction for a criminal offense. The defendant or his[11] counsel could also request referral to Patuxent. Upon an offender's referral to Patuxent, professionals would conduct physical, psychiatric, and psychological examinations of the individual and collect social history information. In a civil proceeding, Patuxent clinical staff would recommend whether the offender was a defective delinquent, and a panel of judges or a jury would decide the issue. It was required that an attorney represent the offender, and the offender could choose a judge or jury trial. If he was found to be a defective delinquent, his criminal sentence was suspended and he began an indeterminate sentence at Patuxent. Otherwise, he was returned to the Division of Correction (or released if his time had expired while under examination at Patuxent).

While at Patuxent, an inmate could have his defective delinquent status reviewed (a re-determination hearing) after two-thirds of his sentence had expired and every three years after that. A Board of

Review was established to monitor inmates' progress annually and operate as the Institution's paroling authority (granting, denying, or revoking conditional release statuses and parole, and recommending release to the community).

The following quote from Report #29 of the Maryland Legislative Council (1950) states the purposes of Patuxent and Article 31-B:

> The primary purpose of such legislation is to protect society from this segment of the criminal population who probably will again commit crimes if released upon expiration of a fixed sentence; and thus they should be detained and specially treated unless and until cured. A secondary purpose is more effectively and humanely to handle them, which aids in the cure, where possible. (Reiblich and Hubbard 1950, 1)

It has been suggested (Carney 1985, CRC Report 1977, Roy circa 1986) that lengthy confinement for defective delinquents, constituting public protection, was foremost in the minds of the framers of Article 31-B, while others (Longmire 1979, Lejins 1977) give credence to the framers' faith in the medical model and suggest that Patuxent really was an experiment in law and psychiatry. The present study did not determine the true and original intent of the law. The language and procedures devoted to evaluation and release of defective delinquents suggest that rehabilitation was in fact seriously considered by the drafters of Article 31-B, but as is often the case, the broad language and provisions of the law left room for punishment- (lengthy confinement) and treatment- (focus on rehabilitation and release) oriented interpretations by legislators and administrators alike.

The Indeterminate Sentence

The indeterminate sentence was at the heart of the philosophy behind Patuxent. Clinicians and correctional administrators alike felt it was a necessary component. They felt it was necessary to preserve public safety. Defective delinquents were defined as dangerous, anti-social, psychopathic offenders, and it was felt they would commit fewer violent offenses if they were incarcerated for long periods of time, longer than the current sentencing structure would permit (Reiblich and Hubbard 1950, 2). Additionally, clinicians at Patuxent felt that the indeterminate sentence was necessary as an external motivator to induce inmates to participate in therapy. Criminal psychopaths were thought to be resistant to therapy, so a voluntary treatment program was not designed.[12]

Coerced Therapy

Participation in therapy was coerced at Patuxent in the sense that an inmate could not hope to attain freedom without participating, and the "defective delinquent" status was imposed and not chosen. Eventually, the nature of the coercion took on many different forms in the eyes of the media, the public, and the legislature. Carney (1985) reproduced the following excerpts from a Baltimore daily paper, the *News American*, June 11, 1974:

> A man can take only so much pressure, (a guard) said, especially psychological pressure. And out here, when a man doesn't go along with the program, they go after him.
>
> Those who break, those who fight the program or those who simply refuse to cooperate, are thrown into isolation areas for months or years. Or they are strapped into canvas restraining sheets for days at a time.
>
> Or they become targets for the goon squad.
>
> The goon squad is about half a dozen guards, and they use their muscle just about every night. They'll go after, say, a militant. A militant can be a loud talker or a guy who just writes his congressman.
>
> They have blackjacks with steel balls in them, and come-along chains and Mace.
>
> When they throw a man in the hole (solitary confinement), they whip his ass. You can't see through the walls. And if the inmate files a complaint, they say he molested an officer." (Carney 1985, 13–14)

This research found no evidence of any official inquiry into any alleged abuses by staff against inmates. It is highly likely that many internal investigations of abuse were conducted by the Patuxent administration, but this research did not investigate that issue. The 1977 Contract Research Corporation (CRC) evaluation of Patuxent refers to interviews held with inmates in a section on "Inmate Attitudes, Observations, and Morale." This section did not mention allegations or discovery of physical abuse of any kind (Contract Research Corporation 1977, 101–105). Nonetheless, early newspaper accounts of practices at Patuxent often made reference to beatings, forced medications, LSD experiments, and other abuses that would have been considered criminal.

The Examination and Hearing Processes

Inmates referred to Patuxent underwent extensive testing and observation, involving at least three clinicians, before a determination of defective delinquency was made. Typically, the examination process lasted four to six months and involved medical, psychiatric, psychological, and educational testing, as well as a social history investigation and interview, and observation of the inmate in individual or group therapy. Following the examination, Patuxent staff made a recommendation to the court (a panel of judges, or a jury, if the defendant requested it or if the judge directed it) regarding defective delinquency in a civil hearing. The defendant was provided a copy of the examination report and, if he did not retain counsel was provided counsel. A finding of defective delinquency resulted in an immediate commitment order to Patuxent for an indeterminate sentence without minimum or maximum limits. If the court determined the defendant was not a defective delinquent, the defendant was returned to custody for the duration of his original criminal sentence. A defendant had the opportunity to request a rehearing. Once that request was exercised, a second or subsequent rehearing was not possible until three years had passed.

Confinement and Release

Confinement at Patuxent was governed by the existing laws and standards for correctional facilities in Maryland, with the exception of the treatment program. As described above, the nature of the treatment program was not mandated. It was the responsibility of the Director and Associate Directors, and it evolved over the years. Release from Patuxent, under any status (day leave, work release, parole), was governed by the Board of Review, Patuxent's inmate review and paroling authority. The Board of Review was comprised of the Director, Associate Directors, and several members of the governing board (the Board of Patuxent Institution, whose members were appointed by the Governor). With minimal guidance from Article 31-B, the Board of Review had the authority to establish its own procedures and conditions for provision and revocation of release statuses.

Thus, the events of the day in Maryland—public and legislative outrage over heinous crimes; the influence of judges, lawyers, and psychiatrists; and confidence in the medical and behavioral sciences, especially regarding diagnosis and treatment of criminal offenders—led to the creation of Patuxent Institution, a correctional treatment facility organized along the medical model, with the following characteristics: definition of a class of offenders, an indeterminate sentence, extensive clinical resources, latitude regarding treatment practices, and control over how treated offenders are released into the community.

Early Experiences

Patuxent spent its first five years under the administrative authority of the Division of Correction. Documented accounts of treatment practices at Patuxent during its early years (1955–1960) are scarce and come primarily from the Patuxent administration, leaving little room for determination of accuracy. The treatment program at Patuxent began as an informal one. Not all inmates were in therapy, and those that were did not necessarily participate in group therapy. The first Director, Dr. Harold M. Boslow, encouraged therapists to select the inmates they wanted to treat, and to use the methods they felt were most appropriate. The exact nature of the therapies practiced (e.g., psychoanalysis, directive, non-directive, art therapy) was not well documented.[13]

An article published in 1959 describing Patuxent contained the following:

- Up to that time, 200 inmates had been committed to Patuxent (over 450 had been diagnosed by professional staff), and the capacity was 386 beds.

- Thirteen had been placed on parole, five who had been returned for "adjustment" problems.

- Six professional staff members were employed (three psychiatrists and three psychologists), along with two consulting professionals (one of each profession).

- Group therapy methods were being explored, as was drug therapy.

- Resistance to therapy was not posing undue administrative problems.

- A research program was under way (Boslow et al. 1959).

When Patuxent opened its doors in January 1955, it did so amidst controversy and virtually without correctional staff (Roy circa 1986, 9). By 1959, the staff numbered 309 (including three shifts of correctional officers).

In addition to the information gleaned from Boslow's 1959 article, the following points are illustrative of this embryonic period:

- Considerable time and energies were devoted to recruiting staff, establishing procedures, and generally setting up the Institution.

- Dr. Boslow was not comfortable with the status of Patuxent Institution as an institution under the control of the Board of Corrections. In Dr. Boslow's mind, the Board was not sufficiently knowledgeable about correctional treatment and the needs of Patuxent Institution to adequately oversee its operations or plan for its needs. Dr. Boslow had to fight for his budget in competition with the other correctional institutions in Maryland.[14]

Patuxent was named in a series of court cases almost from the start, challenging its procedures and constitutionality. One early case challenged that forcing offenders to undergo diagnostic evaluation for admission to Patuxent amounted to double jeopardy. Another challenged that Patuxent was not a "place of confinement," thus an attempted escape from Patuxent should not count against the individual. Others challenged Article 31-B regarding the definition of "defective delinquent," and arguing that it constituted denial of fair trial, denial of equal protection under the law, and cruel and unusual punishment (Roy circa 1986, 5–6).

These and other legal challenges led the Maryland Legislative Council (the body that ordered the original studies of law and psychiatry leading to Patuxent's creation) to appoint the Thomsen Commission (named after Chief Judge of the United States Fourth Circuit Court Roszel C. Thomsen, who chaired the Commission) in 1964 and direct it to study Patuxent. This was the first in a series of investigations into Patuxent. Hearings were held, and witnesses testified to the Committee. Most testimony was favorable to both Patuxent and the indeterminate sentence. The Commission recommended two changes to Article 31-B: (1) change the time between commitment as a defective delinquent and first rehearing from three years to two thirds of the fixed sentence, and (2) move Patuxent out from under the Division of Correction, and create a Governing Board to oversee its operations.

This second change had far reaching consequences for Patuxent, especially for the treatment goal. Though support for Patuxent was expressed in the name of public protection, granting Patuxent independent authority opened the door for the development and refinement of treatment practices. As an institution under the Division of Correction, prior to the Thomsen Commission, Patuxent's administrators had to fight for resources in an organization (the Division of Correction) that had little interest or experience in clinical treatment or psychiatry. Coupled with an expensive operation at Patuxent (a higher annual cost per inmate compared to other Maryland prisons), Patuxent lost many battles for scarce correctional dollars. Testimony on these issues by Patuxent staff and supporters influenced the actions of the Thomsen Commission (Roy circa 1986, 8).

Synopsis

In the precursors to and creation of Patuxent Institution we find an oft-told tale — heinous crimes that outrage the legislature, the public, and justice system professionals, resulting in investigations and legislative action. While not always a formula for success, we witness this sequence of events often, almost as if it has been scripted. Our historical analysis reveals, as well, the social and legal forces at work in the case of Patuxent Institution. There had been a smattering of legislative activity in Maryland and across the country (dating back several decades) regarding "defective delinquents" (individuals with emotional, psychiatric, or psychological problems who are convicted of crimes and in need of both treatment and punishment); several serious murder cases in Maryland (also over a period of about 20 years); and a growing local and national interest in positivist approaches to the treatment of serious criminals, as evidenced by the writings and testimony of Karl Menninger and others. In the more immediate environs of Baltimore, Maryland, we find an activist judge (Ulman) bolstered by leading medical opinion (Guttmacher and colleagues), several state-based study commissions concerned with the serious violent offender, and a legislature willing to appropriate funds for new prison construction. To be sure, Patuxent Institution grew as much from the leading positivist philosophies in our broader social and legal culture as from politics and compromise at the local level. The thinking that supported the creation of Patuxent Institution was in place in the late 1940s, but Patuxent would not have been created without the work of several study commissions and the compromise worked out between them, which resulted in Article 31-B of the Public General Laws of Maryland, Patuxent Institution's enabling legislation.

By 1965, just under 10 years since its inception, Patuxent experienced its first round of legal challenges, administrative difficulties, legislative hearings and investigations that would significantly influence its development as an organization. The first outcome for Patuxent, as the proceedings of the Thomsen Commission and subsequent decisions indicate, supported the treatment program. The stage was set for the program to build and flourish, though the next decade would present its own set of difficulties.

Notes

1. Longmire (1979) describes the M'Naghten case and Standard in detail, pp. 12–25. See also Bazelon (1988) for a federal judge's perspective on the historical development of the insanity plea.

2. Durham was actually overruled and replaced by a new standard in *Brawner v. United States* (1972). Longmire (1979), Pike (circa 1977), and Halleck (1971) provide extensive discussions of M'Naghten and its relation to personality disorders. Bazelon (1988), who wrote the decision for *Durham*, explains that the *Durham* standard was rarely applied outside of his court (the Washington, D.C. Federal Circuit Court), but that the *Durham* decision was influential. According to him, the M'Naghten rule required that it be shown that the defendant suffered from such "a defect of reason, from disease of the mind, as not to know the nature and quality of the act he was doing; or, if he did know it, that he did not know what he was doing was wrong" (p. 30). M'Naghten ignored the modern (1970s) dynamic theories of human personality by concentrating only on cognitive reasoning, and did not allow psychiatrists to testify on the full range of influences on human behavior and responsibility. The Durham rule held that an accused was not criminally responsible if it is shown that "his unlawful act was the product of mental disease or defect" (p. 31).

3. This brief sketch is by no means an adequate legal review of developments since M'Naghten. It is meant to portray a brief historical review of a legal trend that figured in the creation of Patuxent.

4. Duker's accomplice, Dale Lambert, got life.

5. Maryland was not the nation's leader in these matters. In 1921 New York opened the first prison for defective delinquents at

Napanoch, followed soon thereafter by the opening of a special department for mental defectives in Bridgewater, Massachusetts, in 1922. These institutions relied on indeterminate sentences, as did Patuxent later on (Rotman, 1995, p. 179).

6. These are the causes for delay cited by Dr. Francis Carney.

7. The 1920s and 30s were progressive years for psychiatry (Lejins 1977), and it may be that it took a generation for the legal system to catch up.

8. In addition to *Duker*, the *James* case, in which James brutally murdered a young girl and was hanged, was mentioned. So, too, was the *Salinger* case, in which an armed robber and diagnosed "psychopathic personality" was acquitted on grounds of insanity.

9. This historical information was gleaned primarily from the following sources: Research Report # 29 of the Maryland Legislative Council, written by Reiblich and Hubbard, 1950; *The Will to Fail,* the unpublished manuscript of Francis L. Carney, Chief Psychologist at Patuxent Institution; the unpublished dissertation of Dennis R. Longmire, University of Maryland; the "Report of the Commission to Study Medico-Legal Psychiatry," December 1948; and the published opinion of Judge Joseph N. Ulman in the Duker Case.

10. The offender himself could request a referral to Patuxent.

11. At the time, Patuxent was a facility for male inmates only.

12. The issue of coerced treatment was not raised in Research Report No. 29. Francis Carney, in his manuscript, *The Will to Fail,* raises this issue, and it was repeated many times in interviews with clinicians who worked at Patuxent in the early years.

13. This information is based on the author's observations at two different gatherings of Patuxent staff in 1985. One was a luncheon for a parting student intern attended by clinical staff and the researcher, at which three members of the clinical staff described Patuxent in its early days. At another more formal gathering, a bi-weekly staff symposium, two Patuxent staff with many years of clinical experience gave an informal historical presentation of Patuxent.

14. Dr. Jonas Rappaport, former Director of the Medical Office of the Supreme Bench of the Baltimore City Court (the position once held by Manfred Guttmacher), was a consultant to the Maryland Department of Corrections during this time, related in an interview that James W. Curran, then the Commissioner of Corrections, "denuded" Patuxent by holding up staff appointments, withholding resources, and using prison beds for regular inmates. Jerome Robinson, Manfred Guttmacher, and Kenneth Reiblich "rose hell" over this, which resulted in the appointment of the first commission to review Patuxent—The Thomsen Commission.

Chapter Five

Growth and Change: 1960–1969

Patuxent experienced its "golden years" in terms of treatment in the 1960s. Moving the Institution out from under the restrictive administration of the Maryland Division of Correction, plus support from the Maryland legislature, led to growth in resources and in the ability to innovate in the area of treatment. With an independent status, and five years' experience treating defective delinquents, Dr. Boslow and his Associate Directors further developed the treatment program. They developed the graded tier (behavioral modification) and unit treatment team concepts. Most accounts credit Associate Director for Behavioral Sciences Dr. Arthur Kandell for these innovations. They established community-based treatment. They experimented with different treatment modalities (for example, groups for retarded offenders, drug therapies), as well as innovative educational and vocational programs (for example, a barbering school, a speech and audiology clinic with one administrator and inmate volunteers, and a radio service for the blind).

This decade, too, was not without controversy. The civil rights movement extended to prisoners, and this brought some unrest to the Institution. The lawsuits continued. Media and public anti-Patuxent campaigns took form. The criminal justice system began to re-evaluate the concept of responsibility for criminal actions, and the propriety of rehabilitating criminals. Many of these controversies came to a head, locally and nationally, in the early 1970s, the beginning of the end for the defective delinquent statute.

Organizational Development and Legal Challenges

In reality, two principal movements took place during the decade of the 1960s—development of treatment methods and increasing legal intrusion.[1] This chapter reviews the legal and institutional developments that characterized Patuxent during the 1960s, and that led to serious troubles in the 1970s.

The 1969 Annual Report for Patuxent Institution provides the following administrative data:

1. The Institution's capacity was 600.

2. The total operating expenditure for Patuxent in Fiscal Year 1956[2] was $505,147. By Fiscal Year 1969 it was $3,411,933. This represents an average annual increase of approximately 40% in operating expenses, not controlling for inflation, and not including capital expenditures.

3. The average daily population grew from 186 in Fiscal Year 1956 to 498 in Fiscal Year 1969, an average annual increase of 12%. The peak average daily population was reached in Fiscal Year 1969, and this included 357 Defective Delinquents.

4. The per capita cost for Patuxent Institution[3] was listed as $2,716 in Fiscal Year 1956 and $6,846 in Fiscal Year 1969, representing an average annual increase of 11%, not controlling for inflation.

The following data, from the same annual report, reflect activity for the Fiscal Years 1960 to 1969:

5. During those years Patuxent staff diagnosed approximately 170 inmates per year, ranging from a low of 63 (not including the first year 1955, when 9 inmates underwent diagnosis) to a

high of 233. In prior years the number of annual diagnoses averaged about 90 (note: data missing for some years).

6. On average, 74 Defective Delinquent hearings were held in court each year. The average from Fiscal Years 1963 to 1965 peaked at over 100.

7. Patuxent staff testified in approximately 56 Defective Delinquent rehearings per year.

8. Patuxent granted parole to 333 inmates since 1956, averaging 31 paroles per year. Of those 333, 151 had returned, 86 with new offenses, and 65 as technical parole violators.[4]

9. Forty-nine inmates had been released through petition to the Courts, and 131 inmates had been released through "legal technicalities."[5]

The 1969 Annual Report listed 357 staff for Patuxent Institution (Table 2 below).

In a 1961 article authored by Dr. Boslow (Patuxent's first Director) and several of his colleagues from Patuxent, the Patuxent clinical (treatment) staff was described as comprising nine treatment staff: five psychiatrists, three psychologists, and one group (social) worker for approximately 300 inmates (Boslow et al. 1961, Patuxent Institution 1969).[6] In addition one or two senior managerial clinical staff provided treatment or diagnostic services to inmates.[7] This definition does not include medical personnel who were licensed physicians, and who provided medical treatment to inmates.

That same article described the Institution's operations. At that time Patuxent had only one Associate Director, the Superintendent (administratively the equivalent of a prison warden in Maryland). Group therapy was the most widely used treatment modality, and "tier counseling" (large group counseling, generally a meeting with all inmates and treatment unit staff from a cell block or wing) also took place. A graded tier system operated, whereby inmates worked up from tiers with few privileges to tiers with greater privileges, based on good behavior and treatment progress. Disciplinary measures were largely under the control of clinical staff, not custodial staff (correctional officers).

The type of therapy received by an inmate depended upon the therapist he was assigned to. Therapists were encouraged by Dr. Boslow to select the inmates they desired to work with; no random or

Table 2
Patuxent Institution Staff in FY 1969

Occupation	Number of Employees
Clinical Staff:	
Psychiatrists	10
Psychologists	10
Social Workers	14
Educational Staff:	
Academic Instructors	9
Vocational Instructors	9
Recreation Specialists	4
Administrative Staff:	
Medical Personnel	10
Classification Personnel	7
Administrative Personnel	5
Fiscal Personnel	9
Maintenance Personnel	13
Food Service Personnel	8
Clerical Personnel	22
Correctional Staff:	
Correctional Personnel	227
TOTAL	357

systematic assignment procedure was used. Generally there were eight to ten inmates in a therapy group. Boslow mentioned five different types of groups in the article: two groups of sex offenders, one group of borderline psychotics, one group of African Americans,[8] and groups based on IQ (one group of inmates with high IQs and one with low IQ inmates). Clinicians attempted using co-therapists with one group, but discontinued this practice. Boslow also noted that a therapy group run by the social worker was under consideration as a "minor experiment." Dr. Boslow reported that, as expected, inmates committed to Patuxent as Defective Delinquents with indeterminate sentences resisted therapy and the "DD" label strongly at first, but most of them developed an acceptance and desire for therapy over time, to the extent that some expressed extreme disappointment upon finding they were removed from group therapy for any reason (Boslow et al. 1959, Boslow et al. 1961).

Dr. Arthur Kandell, former psychologist and onetime Associate Director for diagnostic services, is generally credited with most of the treatment practices developed for Patuxent and those currently in use.[9] Under his direction, Patuxent established an experimental tier and, in conjunction with Dr. Sigmund Manne (former Chief Psychologist at Patuxent), established the graded tier system, as well as the unit treatment team concept (whereby four separate treatment teams operate as independent units), tier counseling (see above), and a gradual community release system with a halfway house.[10] Dr. Kandell and Dr. Manne remained with Patuxent after the change in Article 31-B in 1976 (Dr. Kandell briefly, Dr. Manne until 1984), but it was during the early and mid-1960s that they (again, working with other clinical staff) developed the treatment programs and procedures that operated up to the present time.

Almost from its inception, Patuxent Institution found itself amidst legal and public controversy. Dean Robert H. Roy (a member of Patuxent's Governing Board from 1961 to 1972), in his unpublished review of Article 31-B, cites the following revealing numbers:

1. In Volume 17 of the Maryland Digest, Defendant Plaintiff Table, the Director of Patuxent was named as the defendant in 156 actions brought by 119 different inmates.

2. Additionally, in a document titled, "Decisions Affecting the Defective Delinquent Statute (Article 31-B)," prepared in three volumes by the Court of Appeals of Maryland (covering 1956–1967), 37 other plaintiff names appear (Roy circa 1986, 5).

The legal troubles faced by Patuxent covered the Institution's operating procedures, constitutionality, the indeterminate sentence, the definition of Defective Delinquents, and indeed a wide range of possible legal challenges. The four court cases reviewed below represent examples of the kinds of legal challenges brought to the courts against Patuxent.

The Eggleston Case

In 1955 Martin H. Eggleston, Jr., was convicted on two counts of larceny and received two concurrent six-month sentences for which he was sent to the Maryland House of Corrections. He was referred to Patuxent from that institution for evaluation as a Defective Delinquent (DD). Patuxent clinical staff diagnosed him as a Defective Delinquent, and the diagnosis was affirmed in court seven months later. He was committed to Patuxent on an indeterminate sentence. Eggleston's lawyer petitioned the sentencing court for his release on two grounds: (1) double jeopardy, Eggleston received two sentences for the same conviction, and (2) when the Court found Eggleston to be a Defective Delinquent, his fixed (criminal) sentence was effectively over and the Court no longer had jurisdiction in the case. His claims were denied, and again denied on appeal.

The Caparella Case

William Caparella had a five-year fixed sentence increased by five years for escaping from Patuxent. His counsel argued that, since Patuxent was not a "place of confinement," as defined in Maryland law, the punishment for escape should not apply. This motion was denied.

The Sas Case

Counsel representing John Sas and four other Patuxent inmates challenged Patuxent on the following grounds: the application of the definition of Defective Delinquent, and the constitutionality of the defective delinquency hearing and procedures. This case was appealed from the Circuit to the United States Fourth District Court. The opinion of the Court in this case favored Patuxent, but it contained language that recommended careful consideration of the defective delinquency statute in light of the grave consequences of a finding of defective delinquency.

The Musgrove Case

Inmate Frank Musgrove refused to be evaluated at Patuxent following a plea of guilty to Storehousebreaking with Intent to Steal. Musgrove's counsel claimed that the interviews required in the evaluation process amounted to forced self-incrimination. Musgrove was released on technicalities, but the Court upheld Patuxent's diagnostic procedure. By this time (1966), however, Musgrove's tactic of refusing evaluation caught on among Patuxent inmates, and much trouble was to come of it.

These are but a few examples of the many legal actions brought against Patuxent from its opening through the 1960s and 1970s. In some instances, the same issues were tried in different Maryland counties, but the results were the same: affirmation of Patuxent's legal standing. Some lower court rulings went against Patuxent, but they were always overturned on appeal (too late, in some instances, to avoid serious trouble and damage). Some of the opinions written in these cases contained clear warnings to Patuxent and the State of Maryland regarding the grave nature of their business and the potential for procedural abuse, while others contained dissenting opinions. In his review article, Dean Roy expressed a sentiment shared by Patuxent staff, administration, and Governing Board members regarding the embattlement of Patuxent:

> As an Associate Member of Patuxent's Governing Board from 1961 to 1972, I gained the impression that the professional staff was in court inordinately often, not only to testify at determination (of defective delinquency) and redetermination hearings as proscribed by law, but, just as often, as defendants in actions brought by counsel on behalf of inmates. (Roy circa 1986, 5)[11]

Operational Challenges

Problems of a more operational nature attracted attention to Patuxent, especially to its treatment function. As time passed releases from Patuxent did not keep pace with admissions, and cell space became scarce. Crowding became an issue at Patuxent. Patuxent's Governing Board expressed concern over this issue, and in 1964 Governor Tawes appointed a commission to examine "input/output" at Patuxent. This commission, called the Commission to Study Changes and Basis of Selection for Patuxent Institution, was chaired once again by Judge Roszel C. Thomsen of the United States Fourth District Court in Baltimore, Maryland. This Commission recommended, among other things, that the basis for admission to Patuxent be susceptibility to treatment, not defective delinquency; that sentences be increased for violent criminals (thus reducing the constant appearances at defective delinquency hearings by Patuxent staff, and assuring lengthy stays); and that Patuxent be moved back under the administration of the Maryland Division of Correction. None of these recommendations was implemented by the Maryland legislature.

In 10 years the inmate population at Patuxent almost tripled (from approximately 150 in 1959 to approximately 500 in 1969; Boslow, Rosenthal, and Gliedman 1959, Patuxent Institution 1969)[12], and Patuxent Institution could boast a sizable clinical staff found in no other prison in America (34 clinical staff for about 350 inmates in treatment, almost one clinician for every 10 inmates, Patuxent Institution 1969). The treatment program developed from tentative beginnings to a refined and formal operation during that time. As the program developed, senior clinicians began to publish about the activities at Patuxent in professional journals. As the program developed, so did its troubles, however. The steady stream of legal challenges to Article 31-B and the procedures and practices at Patuxent continued. In almost every instance, the courts found in favor of Patuxent Institution, but this did not stem the tide of trouble. The 1970s were to prove even more challenging.

Synopsis

The decade from 1960 to 1969 brought several parallel and countervailing influences on Patuxent Institution. While the end of the decade found Patuxent on solid financial and political footing, these developments were the precursors to difficult times ahead. On the national scene, the civil rights movement incorporated the prisoners' rights movement (and the movement for the rights of the mentally ill). The tenets and premises of these broad social movements challenged several of the founding principles on which Patuxent rested, most notably coerced treatment and the indeterminate sentence. Local developments brought increased public attention, increased public scrutiny, and additional lawsuits upon

Patuxent. At the same time, crowding within the facility became a problem, prompting the formation of another commission to study issues at Patuxent. As the decade came to a close, none of these pressures, which might have derailed treatment practices at Patuxent or prompted calls for its closure, were felt strongly by the Patuxent administration. In fact, the treatment program was flourishing — new treatment modalities and group therapies were being tried, the clinical staff grew as the inmate population grew. One could say that the absence of strong and direct challenges to its legitimacy on institutional or managerial grounds was allowing the treatment technology to develop and advance. As the next chapter shows, this state of affairs would soon cease.

Notes

1. James Jacobs, in *Stateville,* describes the gradual intrusion of the legal system into the administration of that maximum-security institution in Illinois during the 1960s. The intrusion described here only briefly reflects the societal developments described by Jacobs—a gradual erosion of the formal boundaries between prisons and their surrounding social systems, of which legal intrusion is one facet.

2. July 1, 1955, through June 30, 1956.

3. Per capita cost is arrived at by dividing total operating costs by average daily population.

4. These figures are not meant to indicate performance on Patuxent's part (recidivism). In this context they are merely operational data.

5. This term was not defined in the 1969 Annual Report for Patuxent Institution.

6. In this paper, treatment staff is defined as professional staff trained in group therapy techniques that provide diagnostic (clinical assessment) and clinical (therapy) services to inmates at Patuxent. These include primarily psychiatrists, psychologists, and social workers, as indicated in the list of Patuxent staff.

7. For example, the prior Executive Directors of Patuxent occasionally provided individual therapy to inmates, and the Associate Director for Behavioral Sciences served on the diagnostic staff in reviewing inmates for admission.

8. Inmates were never segregated by race or ethnicity at Patuxent. This refers to a therapy group of African Americans that met only once a week for a time in the past. Such therapy groups are not formed as a matter of policy at Patuxent.

9. Credited also for contributions to Patuxent's treatment program are other past employees, including Dr. Boslow, Dr. Bob Cherry, Dr. Sigmund Manne, and Dr. David Rosenthal. Dr. Kandell is mentioned most often as the pioneer among these contributors.

10. Much of the information suggesting this attribution of influence to Dr. Kandell and others came from interviews and observations conducted during the course of this research. Few written references attributing such exist.

11. This sentiment was expressed in the 1965 report of the second Thomsen Commission, a legislatively appointed investigative body whose job it was to examine Patuxent's admission practices and criteria.

12. Several reports provide different totals for the Patuxent Institution inmate population during the early years. The estimates for several years before 1960 range from about 150 to about 300. This may reflect different reporting practices (e.g., reporting average

daily population versus year-end count, or reporting the inmate population in treatment versus all incarcerated inmates at Patuxent (e.g., those in treatment and those in diagnostic status). Regardless of the counting methods, it is clear that the Patuxent Institution inmate population grew substantially from 1959 to 1969.

Chapter Six

Turmoil and Change: 1970–1976

In the early 1970s Patuxent entered a tumultuous period, fueled in part by the social unrest and forces of social justice that shaped America in the 1960s, as well as by the ongoing criticism of and challenge to the legitimacy of the Institution. This chapter explains how these forces came into play, and how liberal and conservative forces joined in an unplanned coalition to forever change the Institution.

"Rippervilles" and Other Pressures on Patuxent

Three different but related developments took place in the early to mid-1970s that focused intense criticism on Patuxent Institution, and led to the eventual repeal of Article 31-B as the Defective Delinquent statute and its re-enactment as the Eligible Person statute. The three developments are:

1. Continuing legal problems for Patuxent that resulted in administrative problems, and eventually violence within the Institution.

2. Political problems, principally attacks from conservatives in the legislature, which were joined by attacks from the press and the public.

3. Mounting social change and unrest outside of the prison walls, which had an impact on the inside. This, too, led to unrest at Patuxent, and then to criticism.

Winning the Battles, but Losing the War: the Impact of Court Cases on Patuxent

Chapter Five reviewed four key legal challenges to Patuxent Institution, cases that dated from the 1960s. They challenged Patuxent's constitutionality on numerous grounds, and in every instance, Patuxent's legality and constitutionality were upheld. Some cases were decided against Patuxent in the lower courts, but these decisions were reversed on appeals. One case, *McNeil v. Director* (1971), reached the U.S. Supreme Court. It concerned a "refuser," an inmate who refused to participate in the diagnostic process at Patuxent after being referred by the court (similar to the *Musgrove* case, also reviewed in Chapter Five). Patuxent lost this case and McNeil was ordered released (he had been in diagnostic status at Patuxent for six years, while his criminal sentence was for five years and, with good time credits, he could have been released even sooner).

The net effect of these legal challenges and victories was positive for the Patuxent administration. Surely it enhanced the survival of the Institution, for if the challenges had been successful and Article 31-B found unconstitutional, the Institution may have been closed. In a sense, though, the victories were pyrrhic. Patuxent survived, but the doors were opened for other controversies that lingered and contributed to difficulties. The court cases brought three liabilities to Patuxent:

1. Much state time and resources were devoted to the court cases. This, coupled with the extensive amount of staff time

spent at defective delinquency re-hearings, contributed to Patuxent's reputation as an expensive liability.

2. The legal process opened the doors for extensive examination into Patuxent's practices. In some instances, while a court found in favor of Patuxent, the presiding judge, in his written opinion, would warn of other potential problems with Patuxent, or caution administrators to be careful in their implementation of the law. In effect, inmates were being invited to file other cases to test Patuxent's constitutionality, and the public was being invited to criticize.[1]

3. In the case of "refusers," when lower courts found in favor of Patuxent inmates, administrative headaches were created for Patuxent. The fact that appellate courts reversed lower court decisions was of little help, since lower court findings raised inmates' hopes and expectations. The number of refusers grew and they came to be regarded as a "class" of inmates at Patuxent—heroes, or at least symbols of hope, to the inmate population, and troublemakers to the administration.

As Dr. Carney related in his account of Patuxent (1985), the original "refusers" case, *Musgrove,* was decided in 1966, but refusing continued as a tactic by inmates. *McNeil,* which was decided by the U.S. Supreme Court in 1972, suggests that the problem of "refusers" had not gone away.

"Rippervilles"

Patuxent was always a target for criticism from conservative members of the Maryland legislature. Several of the individuals interviewed for this research recalled in particular a Delegate Docter (from Montgomery County) who sponsored many bills to abolish Patuxent Institution. His tirades against the Institution and his constant calling for its abolition spawned the term "ripperville," used by Patuxent staff to describe legislative and public attacks against the Institution.

It is difficult to place the three prominent groups that rallied against Patuxent—legislators, the media, and citizens—in clearly defined coalitions or networks that worked in a coordinated fashion to criticize Patuxent. A citizens' coalition, Marylanders Against Patuxent (MAP, comprised mostly of inmates' family members), was active and often demonstrated at the Institution. The legislators responded to inmates, MAP and the general public, and to reports and information from Patuxent Institution and state correctional administrators. The press responded to the legislature, inmates, MAP and the general public, and to the Patuxent and correctional administrators. These three sectors, whether pursuing their interests or performing their societal functions, tended to be involved in controversies surrounding Patuxent. While these groups concerned themselves with many different issues concerning Patuxent, the issues can be classified as follows:

- issues concerning the indeterminate sentence and coercive therapy,
- issues concerning Patuxent's costs and resources, and
- issues concerning Patuxent's treatment model and release practices.

Even though the courts had upheld the constitutionality of indeterminate sentences to Patuxent for defective delinquents, Patuxent's critics focused many of their attacks on the indeterminate sentence. If legal, it was still viewed as inhumane, or unjust. There was always a certain (small) percentage of inmates who stayed at

Patuxent longer than their criminal sentence may have kept them in the correctional system. This was a function of the indeterminate sentence, but it was also the product of a particular interpretation of Article 31-B by the clinical staff. Under Article 31-B, it was felt that society was protected adequately from dangerous criminals when they were given long sentences. The dangerous criminals admitted to Patuxent were sometimes those with short sentences, since the clinical staff felt the indeterminate sentence was required to protect society from these defective delinquents.[2] Since length of sentence was factored into the diagnostic decision-making process in this fashion, it was likely that some Patuxent inmates would stay beyond their criminal sentences. Patuxent's critics viewed this as a problem.

Since it was the legislature's job to review the Patuxent budget and make an appropriation every year, criticisms of its costliness came primarily from this sector. Each year, during budget review time, Patuxent's per capita costs would be compared to the per capita costs of other correctional institutions, and each year they would be higher. The officer-to-inmate ratio was higher at Patuxent, and the clinical staff was larger at Patuxent than at any other correctional institution in Maryland. As an autonomous entity, Patuxent had overhead costs, administrative costs, and costs for its parole function that other institutions did not have. Division of Correction overhead and administrative costs were budgeted in the headquarters office, not in correctional institutions; and the Department of Parole and Probation was a separate entity whose costs were not figured into the correctional institution budgets.[3] These arguments notwithstanding, legislators and other observers liked to focus on the "bottom line." The bottom line showed that it cost more to run Patuxent, per inmate, than it cost to run other correctional institutions in Maryland. This finding did not always produce a call to abolish Patuxent, but it did produce calls for a number of inquiries into the costs and practices at Patuxent.

Patuxent's critics often focused on the Institution's release practices and, either directly or by implication, the treatment model.

Typically, publication in the media about an incident involving a Patuxent inmate released to the community raised Patuxent's public profile as well as its vulnerability to criticism from the press and legislature. Such incidents provided strong ammunition for critics.

Social Change and Patuxent Institution

While Patuxent experienced court challenges and public criticisms in state, local, and organizational settings, social change in America was also having its impact on Patuxent. The 1960s and 1970s witnessed many legal and social changes as a result of the civil rights movement. Civil rights were extended to prisoners, and prisoners came to be recognized as a disenfranchised group. Black militancy came to Patuxent, as it came to many prisons across the country. The mentally ill were also being viewed as a special population in need of legal protection. As a result, the major underpinnings of Article 31-B (indeterminate sentence, coerced therapy) came increasingly under criticism.[4] Professionals were changing their minds about positivism and the behavioral sciences as well. Confidence in the effectiveness of treatment began to wane, due both to new developments in the fields of psychiatry, psychology, and social work, and to the lack of any concrete evidence that correctional treatment was working.

The Path to Violence

It was the challenge to Patuxent's legal standing (and hence its legitimacy) represented by the many lawsuits brought against the Institution, not the eventual outcome of the lawsuits, that contributed to the downfall of the defective delinquency law. For the constitutionality and legality of Patuxent's procedures, while found lacking in some county courts in Maryland, were always upheld in appellate courts and eventually in a case that reached the Supreme Court of the

United States. These eventualities were no compensation to those responsible for the day-to-day operation of Patuxent Institution—lower court decrees excited the inmates, the public, and press against Patuxent, and some later reversals contributed to violence and other administrative problems (as inmates who thought they would be freed based on lower court rulings were bitterly disappointed by appellate court reversals). Three legal battles in the early to mid-1970s contributed most heavily to Patuxent's troubles: *McNeil v. Director* (1971), the Miller-Watts hearings, and the "refusers" issue.

"Refusers" refers to inmates at Patuxent who refused to be interviewed or tested for diagnostic purposes after referral to Patuxent. After Musgrove was released (see above) and the idea of refusing caught on, 60 to 70 men refused to be interviewed, and waited for the outcome of another "refusers" case in federal court (*McNeil v. Director*). In *Davis v. Director* (1971), Judge Shearin of Montgomery County freed Davis, whose original sentence had expired, and ordered Patuxent to file a diagnostic report on another refuser whose case was in his court (*Edens v. Director*, 1971), but whose original sentence had not expired.

In response to this order Patuxent sent notes on the behavior of refusers to the court, but did not offer diagnostic evaluations since formal clinical assessments had not been conducted. Some refusers ended up being committed as defective delinquents and some did not. During this time the refusers were still waiting for a decision in *McNeil*. The State of Maryland's appeal in another refuser's case reached the United States Supreme Court in June 1972, but the writ of certiorari was dismissed because the petitioners were no longer at Patuxent. *McNeil v. Director* was decided on the same day, however, in Patuxent's favor but with other serious consequences. McNeil was ordered released from Patuxent, but the blame for the refuser problem was placed on the lower courts, not on Patuxent. In the Supreme Court's opinion, the lower courts should have held refusers in contempt until they agreed to be interviewed by Patuxent staff. In any event, McNeil's release, the most visible result of the case to the inmates, prompted legal actions by more refusers. Judge Shearin ordered another 44 released at a later date, and the Maryland Court of Appeals eventually sent them back to Patuxent. Patuxent could rid itself of neither the refusers nor the problem, and the lower level tiers began to fill up with troublesome inmates.

Patuxent entered the 1970s still feeling the negative impact of the continual legal challenges, and a new development occurred: the arrival of black militant inmates. Dr. Francis Carney (then a clinical psychologist at Patuxent) described the mood:

> Since these men [refusers] weren't in treatment, it wasn't long before the first level tiers became filled to capacity, and they were filled with the most recalcitrant of men. They tended to be behavior problems, and correctional officers found themselves working in an increasingly dangerous situation. The professional staff wasn't much help; the refusers wouldn't talk to us. There was tension in the DC Building [Diagnostic Center], and, as a contagion, it spread to the DD Building [Defective Delinquent Building, where inmates under treatment were housed].
>
> Still, the situation could probably have been managed except that at about this time Patuxent received an influx of black militants, a dangerous and volatile group of men who were violently anti-white and who proclaimed that the Defective Delinquency Law was a racist law designed to lock *black* men up forever. They dichotomized every issue into a black-white struggle, and they were as threatening to white inmates as to white staff.
>
> So there was the active militancy of the blacks and the passive hostility of the refusers, there was racial animosity among the inmates, increasingly repressive tactics by custody, and feelings of helplessness and discontent among the professional staff. In February 1971 Patuxent Institution was an explosion waiting to happen. (Carney 1985, 131–132, emphasis in original text)

In February 1972, after the ruling in the Fourth Federal Circuit Court of Appeals that the Defective Delinquency Law was constitutional, tension and frustration increased among the diagnostic inmates expecting a ruling in their favor. An officer was beaten and taken hostage in the diagnostic building. It took an appearance by then Governor Marvin Mandel, at the demand of the inmates, to secure the officer's release.

On the following morning the inmates in the Defective Delinquent Building dining room staged a sit-in and demanded that Governor Mandel return to Patuxent to talk to them. Governor Mandel refused to appear this time, and eventually the Maryland State Police moved in and took control. Some injuries but no deaths occurred. Dr. Francis Carney described the incident as follows:

> As these men [those in the Defective Delinquent Building] staged their "peaceful demonstration" the rest of the patient population was locked in. Every available correctional officer was then marshaled in the corridors outside the dining room and the kitchen, all decked out in full riot gear, and then Forrest Calhoun [then Associate Director and Superintendent at Patuxent] ordered the inmates to return to their tiers. That wasn't about to work. A more conciliatory approach was then taken, and Lew Smith, Calhoun's Assistant Superintendent and a black man, was sent in to talk to the men. The men respected him, but the Governor had been to the Institution once and the men believed he would come again. The men didn't believe it when they were told the Governor had firmly refused to return.
>
> While all this discussion was going on, the professional staff gathered in little groups in various parts of the Institution. No one from the administration would talk to us, so we listened to rumors and spread rumors of our own, and we magnified every incident. We weren't forbidden to go on the tiers, but it was clear that none of the men would be let out of their cells, officer protection was thin and scattered, the mood of the inmates was uncertain, so none of us was foolish enough to venture out into the Institution. Our fears were fed as more and more State Police arrived, and by noon the Institution was surrounded by them; they carried weapons, and they had huge, vicious dogs.
>
> When negotiations with the inmates broke down, the police moved in, and the end was anticlimactic. The dogs terrified the inmates—and for good reason—so when the dogs moved in the inmates moved out [of the dining hall]. There were a few men in the kitchen work area which was separated from the dining room by a locked grill, they couldn't leave until the grill was unlocked, and what happened then depends on which side you believe. These men contended that they were waiting peacefully to be let out; the police say they resisted and had to be subdued; the men said they didn't fight until after they were attacked. Anyway, there was a fight, some police were injured, and some patients were severely injured. All of these patients were taken down to the hole. (Carney 1985, 139–140)

As tensions at Patuxent increased, events took a racial tone both inside and outside the Institution. Black militant inmates disallowed participation by whites in many activities. A local newspaper, the *Baltimore News American,* adopted the cause of the "black political prisoner" at Patuxent and printed a series of anti-Patuxent articles. Fear on the part of the staff and officers diminished their control of the Institution. Hostile inmates created incidents in the halls and tunnels. In March 1972 a group of diagnostic inmates seized some officers and threatened to kill them, but the situation diffused. Fear and tension mounted. Therapy groups were being canceled, and staff faith in the custodial force waned.

The Miller-Watts Hearings

In July 1972 a number of court cases challenging Patuxent were consolidated into a class action suit, with the hearings held at Patuxent. They came to be called the Miller-Watts hearings, after the two judges who presided over the hearings. The immediate result of the hearings, a number of judicial orders affecting Patuxent, was seen as a victory for inmates. Among other things, Patuxent was ordered to increase bed space, provide treatment to refusers, and offer specific types of treatment. The Patuxent staff and administration ignored the orders, pending appeal, and they were all reversed later. The good that came out of the Miller-Watts hearings was procedural safeguards in the disciplinary process, a ripe forum for abuse of inmates' rights. This change was accepted then and is still a formal part of Patuxent disciplinary procedures.

For a while, the imposition of the Miller-Watts order reduced tension at Patuxent, but in June 1973 the 44 refusers that had been ordered released by Judge Shearin (see above) returned to Patuxent as the result of a successful appeal by the State. In November 1973 ten inmates took the school building over, and one staff member suffered permanent brain damage in the incident. They made 13 formal demands. The State Police broke in, crashing through the wall with a tank. An officer was stabbed as well.

Trouble Continues

In June 1974 there was a "mass escape" from Patuxent (involving six inmates). In July 1974 a young male inmate was killed by another inmate. Officers were injured in both incidents. Four other escapes followed and once again Patuxent found itself the subject of a legislatively mandated investigation.

The following items appeared in the *Baltimore News American* at various times in June 1974:

> Inmates—whom administrators persist in calling "patients"—are strapped into canvas restraining sheets, unable to move any part of their body or head, and are forced to lie in their own excretions for days at a time.
>
> Inmates who have broken rules are locked into dim isolation cells for indefinite periods—some for years—from which they are allowed into the sunlight for a few hours a week.
>
> A "goon squad" of guards, wielding blackjacks, metal chains and Mace, holds reign after dark, conducting its own form of therapy.
>
> Nearly half the Patuxent inmates are kept on a daily diet of drugs, including sedatives, hypnotics and tranquilizers.
>
> Group therapy and other psychological testing have failed miserably. The newspaper obtained copies of rehearsed responses given by inmates to doctors. Inmates call therapy a "sham" and most outside experts agree that therapy can't be forced on a patient.
>
> Bizarre behavior modification experiments have been uncovered. One was electroshock treatments on prisoners, abandoned a few years ago because, as one Patuxent doctor explained, "We caught too much flak on that one."
>
> Another was the injecting of female chromosomes into a prisoner who doctors found to have an extra male chromosome. . . . Patuxent's board of review dropped the project in secrecy and never released the results of the test.[5]

This bad press, with all the other troubles and pressures working on Patuxent, led Dr. Boslow to retire in the summer of 1975. He was replaced by J. Brown Hardy, who was appointed as Acting Director of Patuxent and who ran the Institution when the 1976 Maryland legislative session began. In that session the Contract Research Corporation, the research firm commissioned for the third study of Patuxent, presented its investigative report on Patuxent, and testimony was heard regarding the Institution. Based on this input, and on the many troublesome incidents at Patuxent, Article 31-B was repealed and reenacted.

Synopsis

Our analysis of Patuxent Institution in the 1970s provides an excellent example not only of how organization-environment interactions develop over time and contribute to organizational legitimacy problems, but also of how issues at organizational boundaries have profound impacts on the internal, technical workings of organizations. This issue is profoundly felt by public organizations, especially prisons.

In the case of Patuxent Institution, legal challenges and battles that developed in the prior decade lingered in the 1970s with devastating effects. The "refusers" issue illustrates this point. Inmates began refusing to participate in Patuxent's diagnostic process in the early to mid-1960s, and several cases went to local courts in Maryland. The lower courts decided in favor of the inmates, prompting their release and encouraging other inmates to refuse participation. The State appealed the lower court decisions and eventually won, resulting in the return of some inmates to Patuxent. The net effect of these actions over the course of several years was anger and confusion on all sides (inmate and staff/administration). Related developments include the following — increased public and press criticism of Patuxent (including some damning and never proven allegations of brutality), including demonstrations against Patuxent by citizen groups; attempts by conservative legislators to close Patuxent, and escapes and other forms of unrest (and violence) at Patuxent. Recall that during the late 1960s and early 1970s social unrest in this country (relating to civil rights) was at its peak. All of these developments led the Maryland legislature to commission a research evaluation of Patuxent Institution by an outside research corporation.

Here again, we see the combination, or coalescing, of national movements (our political and legal culture) and local events surrounding Patuxent. In this instance, however, the result is negative rather than positive. The combination of public, press, and governmental questioning of Patuxent's legitimacy produces yet another formal inquiry, with serious consequences.

Notes

1. In *Sas v. Maryland,* 334 F. 2d 506 (4th Cir. 1964) the following language appeared in the opinion:

> [Article 31-B] is so serious a departure from traditional concepts of justice that it deserves a critical analysis on the broadest terms after a careful factual development of its present operation.

In *Tippet v. State of Maryland, and Director of Patuxent Institution,* 436 F. 2d 1153 (4th Cir., 1971), which found for Patuxent, Judge Sobeloff filed a separate opinion concurring in part and dissenting in part, and ended his opinion with the following:

> I venture now to add a word of admonition to the officials of the Institution. In formulating and executing institutional policies the administrators should defer to traditional standards of fair procedure prized, even though not specifically commanded, by the courts. The officials' aim should not be minimal compliance to escape judicial condemnation, but maximum compliance with the spirit and essence of the Bill of Rights protection. Present policies and practices should be

thoroughly examined by them in light of these principles. Administered with this unstinting attitude, the Institution's still experimental program will the more likely progress smoothly and meet with general satisfaction.

2. One former Associate Director at Patuxent pointed this out to me, and it was repeated in other interviews. Some respondents also expressed a belief that some judges "hid behind" Article 31-B, since they could give short sentences to inmates who they could refer to Patuxent if they felt confident they would be diagnosed as defective delinquents.

3. In essence, Patuxent operated a mini-correctional system (admissions, custody and treatment, plus release and parole), and the legislature would compare it to a conventional prison, which did not have the same costs (no admissions/diagnostics, no parole). Patuxent administrators always felt this was an unfair comparison.

4. It is interesting to note that while the ACLU was active in many of these issues, it did not play a prominent role in the legal challenges to Patuxent. At one time, however, a number of Patuxent's governing board members were members of the Maryland ACLU chapter. As the ACLU became more and more outspoken against the indeterminate sentence and other justice system abuses, tensions arose among Board members. One Board member reputedly resigned from the local chapter over this matter.

5. In his account, Dr. Francis Carney admits to "a kernel of truth" in some of these stories, though not those regarding shock therapy and chromosome experiments. Restraining sheets were used, but always under the direction of a physician. Drugs were administered, but only with an inmate's consent, and at the time this practice was common in American corrections. According to

Carney, "goon squad" was the slang name given to Patuxent correctional officers who responded to violent incidents (commonly called the Utility Squad); there was never a "terror squad" that roamed the tiers at night.

Chapter Seven

The Rebirth of Patuxent: 1977–1987

In 1976, on the eve of the most dramatic changes the Institution had ever undergone, Patuxent had grown slightly from 1969. The Patuxent Institution Annual Report for Fiscal Years 1973–1975 presented the following information:

- The average daily population was 506[1] in 1970 and 493 in 1973, peaking in 1972 at 550, and lowest in 1974 at 388.

- The greatest number of inmate examinations occurred in 1970, 148, with the lowest, 58, in 1976. The average over the seven-year period was 120 defective delinquency examinations per year.

- In 1970 Patuxent clinical staff attended 125 defective delinquency hearings or re-hearings, and 97 such hearings in 1976. In 1972 they attended 161 such hearings.

- From 1970 to 1976, the Board of Review granted parole to 396 inmates.

- In 1970 the per capita cost per Patuxent inmate was $7,703. In 1976 it was $11,827 (unadjusted, Patuxent Institution, 1976).

In July 1977, Patuxent Institution began a new era, perhaps best described as a rebirth, though controversy and legitimacy issues were never far removed. The "new Patuxent Institution" began operations on July 1, 1977.[2] The new Article 31-B made no reference to Defective

Delinquents. The law described "Eligible Persons," referring to inmates who met the following criteria, making them "eligible" for treatment at Patuxent:

1. They must be serving a term of incarceration for at least three years, or have at least three years remaining to be served.

2. They must be emotionally unbalanced or intellectually deficient or both.

3. They must be able to profit by use of the programs at Patuxent.

4. They would be better rehabilitated at Patuxent than by other incarceration.

Additionally, they must opt for treatment at Patuxent; a judge, attorney, or correctional official may refer them, but they may not be forced to undergo treatment, and they may request transfer to Patuxent on their own. There was no indeterminate sentence; inmates could not be kept in treatment longer than their criminal sentence. There was no diagnosis of defective delinquency with a subsequent court trial.

The New Patuxent: 1977–1985

Under the revised Article 31-B, Patuxent remained a maximum security correctional institution separate from the Maryland Division of Correction (and still retained its admissions, paroling, and release authority). The indeterminate sentence no longer existed, and clinical treatment continued in much the same way as it had in prior years. The following description of Patuxent's operations was excerpted from the Patuxent Institution Annual Report for Fiscal Year 1986.

> Inmates approved for transfer to Patuxent by the Commissioner [of Corrections] reside in the Patuxent Annex (a double-celled portion of living units used for Division of Correction inmates awaiting evaluation) until living space becomes available in Patuxent's evaluation population. Inmates who "drop into" Patuxent's evaluation population are randomly assigned to one of four separate treatment units, and an elaborate six-month diagnostic procedure begins.
>
> Social workers, psychologists, psychiatrists, correctional officers, education and medical staff examine and observe inmates during the six-month evaluation. Based on formal social history reports; psychological, psychiatric, and medical testing; an educational evaluation; and on staff judgments of inmates' responses to, and motivation for, therapeutic treatment, a panel of clinical staff members evaluates each inmate as an Eligible Person (EP) or Non-Eligible Person (Non-EP). Non-EP's return to the Division of Correction, and may reapply to Patuxent Institution after a three-year period. EP's begin participation in the full treatment program at Patuxent Institution.
>
> Treatment at Patuxent includes a wide range of programs, including psychotherapy, academic (remedial, high school, and college-level) education, vocational training, job training and supervision, and recreation and leisure activities.
>
> A graduated tier and privilege system forms the core of the treatment program...As inmates exhibit continued socially desirable and infraction-free behavior, they move upward in the graded tier system...Staff determine whether an inmate is promoted or demoted to the various levels, and may recommend that the Board of Review find the inmate to be a Non-EP. A finding of Non-EP by the Board of Review returns the inmate to the Division of Correction.
>
> Inmates who successfully reach Level Four [the highest level within Patuxent's walls] prepare for graduated release from Patuxent, beginning with accompanied or unaccompanied single day leaves and progressing through extended leaves, work or school release, parole, and eventual complete release. (Patuxent Institution 1987, 5–8)

By the early 1980s, the politics surrounding Patuxent Institution had settled down a bit, and treatment was the order of the day, still. Various Patuxent Institution Annual Reports between Fiscal Years 1981 and 1986 provide the following data:

1. In Fiscal Year 1979, Patuxent clinical staff evaluated 267 inmates and admitted less than 40% as Eligible Persons. In Fiscal Year 1986, 321 inmates were evaluated with 25% being found to be Eligible Persons, the lowest acceptance percentage since Fiscal Year 1977.

2. In Fiscal Year 1986 the Patuxent staff numbered 411 (Table 3 below).

3. The average daily population in Fiscal Year 1978 was just under 400, reached its peak at over 750 in Fiscal Year 1984, and declined to just fewer than 700 in Fiscal Year 1986.

The annual per capita cost for Patuxent in Fiscal Year 1978 was reported at just under $15,000, and rose to just over $16,000 in Fiscal Year 1986.[3]

The revision of Article 31-B and creation of the new Patuxent did not spell an end to the Institution's troubles, however. Patuxent had always been a controversial correctional institution, and the question was not whether there would be controversy, rather what form it would take. With civil rights and procedural issues put to rest, critical attention turned to economic arguments, and philosophical arguments never ceased.

In 1982 the Secretary of Public Safety and Correctional Services, Thomas Schmidt, attempted to have Patuxent returned to the administrative control of the Division of Correction. This attempt did not succeed, but in the outcome of the struggle Patuxent's Director, Dr. Norma Gluckstern, agreed to double-cell inmates at Patuxent to ease crowding problems in the Division of Correction. As cell space filled up and the average daily population reached its peak in 1983–1984, Patuxent lost some flexibility in assigning living units that is critical to a graded tier system.

Table 3
Patuxent Institution Staff in FY 1986

Occupation	Number of Employees
Clinical Staff:	
Psychiatrists	3
Psychologists	11
Social Workers	16
Re-Entry Program Personnel	9[(a)]
Educational Staff:	
Academic Instructors	9
Vocational Instructors	10
Recreation Specialists	5
Administrative Staff:	
Medical Personnel	7
Records-Data Processing	3
Administrative Personnel	9
Fiscal Personnel	10
Maintenance Personnel	17
Food Service Personnel	13
Clerical Personnel	20
Correctional Staff:	
Correctional Personnel	269
TOTAL	411

(a) Refers to halfway house personnel.

The brutal rape, murder, and burning of Stephanie Ann Roper (age 22) in Maryland in April 1982 brought the victims' rights movement to the State, and its impact was felt on Patuxent. Successful lobbying by victims' advocates (headed by the Stephanie Roper Committee, chaired by Stephanie's mother) resulted in a change to parole practices in Maryland: parole for inmates with life sentences can be granted only by the Governor. The effect on Patuxent was felt in two ways: (1) Lifers on work release stayed there longer and occupied scarce halfway house beds that other Patuxent inmates (non-lifers) might fill, and (2) Delays in granting of parole interfered with treatment plans and progress.

Analyzing the Death and Rebirth of Patuxent in 1977

From approximately 1970 to 1976, the three pressures described in the previous chapters (legal actions against Patuxent, militancy and violence within the prison walls, mounting public criticism) operated on Patuxent Institution, and cast the Institution in a negative light. In 1976, Governor Marvin Mandel, to put an end to the bickering, had the Department of Public Safety and Correctional Services commission a study to evaluate Patuxent. The study was presented by the Contract Research Corporation in February 1977. It recommended radical restructuring of Patuxent's practices and was the basis for a new version of Article 31-B passed by the Maryland legislature that year. Following is a review of the sequence of events leading up to the rebirth of Patuxent under the Eligible Person statute.[4]

To relate the sequence of events leading up to the repeal of the defective delinquent statute, we must return to events surrounding Patuxent in the early 1970s.

1971–1976: Incidents and Developments at Patuxent

The problem of "refusers" as well as a black militancy movement emerged at Patuxent. On February 4, 1971, the Federal Fourth Circuit Court of Appeals handed down its decision in the *Tippett* case (1971), affirming the constitutionality of Patuxent.[5] This decision had a dual affect on Patuxent inmates—those in treatment (in the DD [defective delinquent] building were relieved, and the refusers (in the separate DC [diagnostic center] building) were devastated.

On February 21, 1971, a group of about 10 inmates from the DD building took a guard hostage and beat him.[6] State Police were called to Patuxent, and Governor Marvin Mandel came to the Institution to talk with the inmates. After about 20 minutes, Governor Mandel secured the release of the officer after promising to hear inmates' grievances and to visit with the inmates on M-1 (seclusion), who other inmates claimed were being beaten. While this appeared to defuse the situation, other inmates joined the movement, as Dr. Carney explained:

> Governor Mandel's concern is to be applauded, but he made a mistake. Once the inmates thought they had him on the run, they tried to keep him running. That's what the disturbance the next morning was all about: they wanted the Governor back. This time the Governor refused. (Carney 1985, 138)

On February 22, a larger group of inmates staged a non-violent sit-in demonstration in the Defective Delinquent Building dining hall. They, too, wanted to present their grievances to the Governor. These concerned the indeterminate sentence, poor medical attention, and abuse by correctional officers. Governor Mandel refused to go back in, and negotiations ceased. State Police entered the dining hall with weapons and attack dogs, and the inmates dispersed. They were put in seclusion and eventually tried in absentia and given 15 days confinement in their cells. A fight broke out between the police and some of the kitchen workers (who were not involved in the sit-in), with injuries on both sides. These men were given 90 days solitary confinement. Patuxent returned to "business as usual" the next day, but things were never quite the same due to the recent violent incidents. The inmates under treatment were resentful at the administration and the police for turning a peaceful demonstration into a violent confrontation. The administration, especially the correctional officers, was wary and mistrustful of the inmates. The clinical staff was uneasy, and could also feel the tension.

Soon after the hostage taking and sit-in, custodial staff demanded that certain "agitators" be removed from their cells and isolated from the treatment program. The clinicians protested, but the administration removed the men, fueling rather than defusing the tense situation.

A second hostage taking took place in March 1971. Again the inmates demanded to see Governor Mandel and again he refused. He sent the Secretary of Public Safety, Robert J. Lalley, in his stead, and a reporter from the *Baltimore Afro American*. This proved effective and the hostages (two correctional officers) were released. A few days later another sit-in occurred in the gymnasium. This one ended peacefully, but things were not peaceful. Dr. Carney recalls the mood:

> Day after day it went on like that. Always some new incident, sometimes major, sometimes trifling, but every day brought some new emergency. Would it never come to an end, we wondered. What next?
>
> And nothing happened but the waiting, and the fear became as a palpable thing...Custody became afraid, and no one appreciated that more quickly than the inmates. They began by disregarding some of the minor rules and regulations, and no one said a word to them about it; they began going through the grills and wandering all over the Institution without authorization; the number of available weapons began to multiply, and the stronger inmates began to terrorize the weaker with impunity...Rumors were rampant that a major rebellion was coming. (Carney 1985, 148)

As summer approached, things settled down at Patuxent. This was due in large part to activity in the courts. A number of inmates had filed cases against Patuxent in the Howard and Montgomery County courts. These cases were eventually consolidated into a class action suit, with Julian Tepper (a nationally known civil rights lawyer) defending the inmates. Two judges—Miller from Montgomery County and Watts from Baltimore City—were appointed to hear the case. The hearings were held at Patuxent Institution, an unusual proceeding.[7] The "Miller-Watts trial," as it came to be known, resulted in a number of orders for the Patuxent administration, most of which were impossible or unrealistic. They were ordered to hire more staff, which they could not do without legislative action. They were ordered to provide treatment to refusers, which they could not do legally. They were ordered to start a methadone maintenance program, which the clinicians thought was unwise. They were also ordered to improve the procedures for hearing and deciding punishments for disciplinary infractions, which the clinicians supported. In any event, most of the orders were put on hold pending appeal. The appeals court found in favor of Patuxent, too late to prevent the negative impact of giving the inmates the impression they had power over the administration, via the courts. Things did calm down for a while.

No major incidents happened for a few years, but minor ones kept cropping up. Individual acts of violence took place and lawsuits continued. The press and MAP (Marylanders Against Patuxent) kept the pressure on. Two inmates who had been terminally ill (one with cancer and one with a brain tumor) died. The inmates seized upon this as a new rallying cry against the administration. Most of the incidents that took place lacked any racial context, but eventually the black militant inmates asserted their influence. They declared themselves political prisoners, enlisted the interest and support of the *Baltimore Afro American* newspaper, and of local civil libertarians who joined in the anti-Patuxent movement.

In December 1971, Judge Shearin from Montgomery County handed down a decision in a refusers case that forced the Patuxent administration to submit reports for defective delinquency hearings on approximately 70 inmates, even if they refused to talk to the clinicians. As a result of that decision, some inmates were sent back to the Department of Corrections outright, and the others had their hearings. Some were found to be defective delinquents and came back to Patuxent; others were sent back to the Department of Corrections to finish their sentences. In early 1972, the U.S. Supreme Court ordered Patuxent to release a refuser named McNeil. The opinion, however, faulted the lower courts for their handling of the refusers issue, not Patuxent. Regardless, the refusers saw McNeil go free. Their hopes rose, and more calm was restored to Patuxent.

In June 1973, the Maryland Court of Appeals reversed Judge Shearin's decision on the refusers, and 44 refusers were returned to

Patuxent from the Department of Corrections. As Dr. Carney stated, "...[Patuxent's] respite from turmoil was over."

In November 1973, the most violent uprising in Patuxent's history took place. Ten inmates held a number of teachers hostage in the school building. One was seriously, and as it turned out, permanently, injured with brain damage and an officer received multiple stab wounds. The ten inmates gave the other inmates in the building an opportunity to join or leave and they all left. The hostages issued a number of demands including release of all inmates held at Patuxent beyond the term of their criminal sentences; investigation into medical, custody, and administrative practices; release of all inmates held in seclusion over 30 days; transfer out of the Institution of all inmates under 21; more access to reform programs geared toward black inmates; a stoppage of experimental medical programs that paid inmates $13.00 a month; and others covering diet, religious services, and health care. Negotiations failed and eventually the National Guard and the State Police broke through the school building wall with an armored vehicle, tear gas, and dogs and took control of the building. A number of teachers received minor injuries. Shortly after this incident, Secretary Lally ordered an investigation of Patuxent Institution. In June 1974 six inmates overpowered a guard and escaped. In July a 22-year-old inmate was killed by another inmate. In the same month four other inmates escaped, and two were caught days later in an armed robbery following a high speed chase in which a motorcyclist was killed. In each of these incidents there were injuries of some sort to officers or inmates.

Dr. Carney points out that in all of the violent incidents at Patuxent, there were never more than a few inmates involved. These incidents, however, placed Patuxent in a negative light in the eyes of almost everyone outside of the Institution. Dr. Carney wrote:

> It seemed there was always something to keep Patuxent before the public, and the issues raised by the Institution were debated at the highest levels of professional competence in both the legal and medical professions, but it wasn't the voice of the scholars which was heard. The strident voices were heard. The Coalition Against Patuxent focused on the emotional issues, that

> melodrama which is intrinsically a part of the criminal justice process and the fact of incarceration, and certain newspapers resorted to sensationalism. (Carney 1985, 171)

On July 23, the investigative hearings ordered by Secretary Lally began. The following groups, which had organized themselves into the Coalition Against Patuxent, appeared to testify against Patuxent:

Prisoners' Aid Association
National VISTA Alliance
Baltimore ACLU
Marylanders Against Patuxent
D.C. Black Assembly Legal Injustice Committee
University of Maryland Black Students Union
Maryland Black Students Coalition
ACLU National Prison Project

Many of the charges made were based on newspaper accounts from the *News American*, few facts were presented, and many of the charges were dismissed as unfounded (Carney 1985, 173).

Dr. Boslow retired in the summer of 1975. Article 31-B was revised to allow a non-physician to serve as the Director. J. Brown Hardy, a former social worker at Patuxent and administrator in the Division of Correction, was appointed to replace Dr. Boslow. He proved a capable administrator, and again things quieted down at Patuxent.

The years of turmoil, violent incidents, lawsuits, bad press, citizen outrage, and attacks from conservative legislators had taken their toll, however. The lawsuits, investigations, and changes in Article 31-B eroded some of Patuxent's autonomy, and its reputation was at an all-time low in 1975. Legislation was introduced again to abolish Patuxent and return the facility to the Division of Correction. This time, the legislation passed the House side, but was stalled in the Senate. In this instance, Governor Marvin Mandel intervened and ordered the Department of Public Safety to commission an independent evaluation of Patuxent. The first full-scale assessment of Patuxent was undertaken.

A competitive bid process resulted in the awarding of the research contract to Contract Research Corporation, a consulting firm from Massachusetts. A seven-month study ensued, the results of which were published in February 1977. It was an extensive study covering treatment effectiveness and cost effectiveness issues, relying on numerous data sources and analytical techniques. The following excerpt from the study's "Executive Summary" relates the study team's recommendations:

> Based on scrutiny of both the theory and the practice behind the Institution, this report concludes that the indeterminate sentence and the concept of defective delinquency should be repealed and that the present program at Patuxent should be significantly modified. (Contract Research Corporation 1977, i)

Related Developments in the Reshaping of Patuxent Institution

There was another separate sphere of activity under way in Maryland concerning violent criminals and their treatment. It was taking place under the auspices of the state executive, Governor Mandel, and, as is almost always the case, it was sparked by a heinous crime that received high visibility. Arthur Goode was a pedophile who had been in and out of Maryland's correctional and mental health institutions, and who always seemed to fall through the cracks. He eventually made his way to Florida, where he raped and murdered a young girl, a crime for which he was eventually executed. Having come from Maryland, the Arthur Goode case caused considerable concern and embarrassment. In response to these events, Governor Mandel appointed a task force on aggressive offenders to study the problem and treatment options in mental health and corrections. Jonas Rappaport, then in the Medical Office of the Supreme Bench of the Baltimore City Court (the office once held by Manfred Guttmacher, one of the original designers of Patuxent) and an appointed member of the Board of Patuxent Institution, was a member of the commission, which contained other high-level officials from criminal justice and mental health agencies in Maryland. The Commission was chaired by Alan Wilner, at that time the Chief Legislative Officer on Governor Mandel's staff.[8] Wilner's commission was conducting inquiries and hearings into issues directly relevant to Patuxent—the treatment of aggressive criminal offenders—at the same time that the legislature was considering abolition of the Institution.

Having determined that a treatment approach was necessary to deal with offenders like Goode, and that Patuxent was in danger of being abolished, Wilner took interest in legislative issues surrounding Patuxent and in the CRC study.[9] On behalf of Governor Mandel, he intervened in the debate over Patuxent and took decisive action. At around the time the CRC study was being completed (1976–77), the Senate introduced a companion bill to the one introduced in the House, with 30 sponsors, to abolish Patuxent.

Alan Wilner pursued two extremely effective courses of action. First, he read the draft CRC report, found it to be biased against Patuxent, too focused on philosophical debates about medical models, flawed in its presentation and its methodology, and counterproductive to the Governor's agenda for treating aggressive offenders. Wilner called some members of the CRC study team, staff from Patuxent, and from state government to discuss the draft report. Wilner recounted the meeting as follows:

> ...and I said, "Look, number one I had no problem with your conclusions to a, b, c, d, and e, but you turn in a report like this ...you're going to get scalped, because there's going to be a big fight in the legislature and...you may win the day, but your not going to look too well in your profession when this thing gets torn apart." You know, we just pointed out, "Look where you said this on page 22, but look at what you said on page 65, the exact opposite. How can you reach two opposite conclusions? Which one do you mean? What are you using to support the other one?" [Note: Wilner's reference to the letters a, b, c, etc., and to page numbers were for examples only; they bear no relation to actual items in the CRC report]...I think to some extent, they got shaken up enough that when we came in and said,

> "Look, we'll meet your principal objections. We'll do away with the indeterminate sentence...but you can't really demonstrate that the medical model doesn't work, if it's done properly. All you can demonstrate is that this one doesn't work, and we agree with that." And so, in about three or four days they rewrote large parts of the report...They rewrote a number of their conclusions, and ended up supporting our bill. (Interview with Judge Alan Wilner, January 15, 1987)

Wilner also met with Board of Patuxent members and the Patuxent administration and worked out a new version of Article 31-B, the version that eventually became the Eligible Person statute. The bill was introduced as an administration (Governor's) bill in the House, after which the Senate bill to abolish Patuxent died in committee. Article 31-B passed with hardly any opposition, and the new Patuxent Institution was born in 1977.

The Eligible Person statute did not remove the conflict and controversy surrounding Patuxent Institution; it changed their focus and intensity. With the indeterminate sentence gone and the installment of a voluntary treatment program, violence nearly vanished from inside the prison's walls, and the public outcry was silenced. The next 10 years were good years for the treatment program at Patuxent. It remained almost entirely untouched by the controversy and change that dogged the administration in the past. On any given day, group therapy was conducted with inmates in much the same way that it had been since 1960. A new diagnostic process was implemented and defective delinquency hearings were eliminated, but the clinical diagnostic procedure was much the same. An inmate would spend four to six months in diagnostic status undergoing various tests and observations. An internal "Diagnostic Staffing," in which a team consisting of clinicians and the Associate Directors would review clinical recommendations regarding an inmate's classification as an Eligible Person, replaced the defective delinquency hearings and re-hearings that took up so much of staff time under the Defective Delinquency law. Patuxent retained its community release and paroling authority under the Eligible Person law, so the Board of Review procedure remained almost as it always had been.

What did change was the inmate population under treatment. Dr. Francis Carney compared a cohort of Defective Delinquents with one of Eligible Persons and found them to be comparable on age and IQ variables, but different on four other variables. Eligible Persons had longer criminal sentences, on average over three times as long as was found with Defective Delinquents. Eligible Persons were much more likely to be sentenced for the violent crimes of murder, rape, assault, or robbery, but were much less likely to have prior criminal convictions. Finally, black inmates constituted 58% of the Eligible Person cohort and 40% of the Defective Delinquent cohort (Carney 1989, 8).[10] It appears that Patuxent inmates under the Eligible Person statute were more violent, but less criminally prone, than Defective Delinquents.

Dr. Carney also considered the psychiatric characteristics of the two populations. Lack of any consistent diagnostic data across the Defective Delinquent and Eligible Person populations makes a comparison of their psycho-dynamics difficult. Dr. Carney relied on his extensive experience treating inmates under both laws, and on some of the early writings of Dr. Boslow, to make the following comparison:

> Generally, the **average** DD and the **average** EP are probably more alike than different. It's only when we get away from the **average** that we see the difference between the two populations: the extreme DD was in fact severely amoral and unresponsive to any treatment intervention, and the extreme EP is psychodynamically noncriminal though he committed a criminal act. (Carney 1989, 11)

With a new law and a new inmate population, Patuxent began a new life and a new era. Violence was nearly eliminated but controversy was not. As always, there were conservative legislators who stirred things up in the legislature each year, especially during budget hearings. Citizen activism continued with the rise of the victims' rights movement (for which there was a strong advocate in

Maryland). And there was always the occasional relapse into criminal activity of an inmate on release from Patuxent. Patuxent's status and history ensured that these would be reported in the press more often than not, while similar incidents with Division of Correction inmates received less publicity. Patuxent's next serious challenge came from within the Department of Public Safety, though, not as a direct result of violence, escapes, or public outrage. It came from state agency competition over resources.

Conflict over Resources

Patuxent Institution served under one Secretary of Public Safety and Correctional Services under the Defective Delinquent statute, Robert J. Lally, and has served under more than five Secretaries under the Eligible Person statute.[11] Lally had been a personal friend of Dr. Boslow's; their acquaintance began years before Patuxent opened, when Lally was with the FBI. While not a clinician, Lally was sensitive to Dr. Boslow's needs and the difficult time he was having at Patuxent. This did not prevent him from conducting inquiries into Patuxent, as he did in 1973. Governor Agnew appointed Gordon Kamka as Secretary when he took office in 1978. Kamka was known as being sympathetic to Patuxent, and he supported the appointment of Dr. Norma Gluckstern as Director in 1979. Thomas W. Schmidt was appointed by Governor Hughes, and was later replaced by Frank Hall. Schmidt was from state government, having served as a budget analyst in many capacities and eventually as the head of the State Budget Bureau. He served as Secretary for approximately two years. Frank Hall came from outside the state, from Massachusetts. He was something of a well-known and controversial figure, having shut down all of the juvenile correctional facilities while directing that state's juvenile correctional system. He left Maryland around the time that Hughes' term was coming to an end, and was replaced temporarily by Calvin Lightfoot, the Deputy Secretary. Governor

Schaffer, upon his election in 1986, named Baltimore City Police Chief Bishop Robinson Secretary, who served in that capacity for about 10 years. Of all these Secretaries, only Schmidt was known as a detractor of Patuxent. It was under his administration that conflict over resources came to a head.

As a correctional institution separate from the Division of Correction, and with paroling authority separate from the Division of Parole and Probation or the Parole Commission, Patuxent was always vulnerable to criticisms from within the ranks of the Maryland criminal justice system. The Director of Patuxent Institution was on equal footing with the Commissioners of Corrections and Parole, though the size of the operation was quite small in comparison, and had equal access to the Secretary. The relationship of the Director of Patuxent to the Secretary of Public Safety and Correctional Services, then, was a critical one for the survival of Patuxent Institution. The Secretary could be protective and supportive, or could be non-supportive to the point of being antagonistic. Similar situations exist in nearly all state governments, but no other state has a Patuxent. With its own legislative mandate to treat criminals, its independent status, the ebb and flow of controversy surrounding its practices, Patuxent was in a unique and vulnerable situation.

In 1982 Maryland, like many states, faced a severe problem with crowding in its correctional institutions, and there was no desire on the executive or legislative side to build more prisons. This forced Secretary Schmidt, who came up through the ranks as a budget analyst, to take a critical look at all the resources under his command—both facilities (bed space) and finances. In 1981, Patuxent's average daily population was 580 (Patuxent Institution 1982, 17). The design capacity was 640, and no inmates were double-celled.[12] Thus, in the eyes of Secretary Schmidt, there were approximately 60 beds at Patuxent that were not being used, and no inmates were double-celled. There were no free beds in any other correctional facility, and he was being forced to increase the rate of double-celling in nearly all of them. In addition, the financial numbers showed that Patuxent cost more to operate than the other prisons. In 1982, the per capita annual inmate cost at Patuxent was $4,000 to $5,000 more than either the Maryland Penitentiary or the Maryland House of Corrections, two maximum security institutions (Patuxent Institution 1985, 15).[13]

Norma Gluckstern, then the Director of Patuxent Institution, learned that Secretary Schmidt was preparing to make an argument at the upcoming legislative budget hearings before the Committee on Public Safety and Transportation for placing Patuxent back under the administration of the Division of Correction, primarily as a means of securing desperately needed beds for Division inmates, and as a means of reducing the cost of corrections in the State of Maryland. Dr. Gluckstern argued vehemently against such a move, mostly in private conversations with Secretary Schmidt, other state government officials, and with legislators in Annapolis. She found herself in a struggle to counter the decisions of her superior.

Eventually, she proposed a compromise to Secretary Schmidt and the House Committee. To help the Division of Correction with its crowding problem, and to maintain the autonomy of the Institution, she offered to double-cell a portion of the DC building, where inmates lived in diagnostic, not treatment, status. She could house close to 200 inmates with this change she argued, and not seriously compromise the treatment program. The proposal was accepted. In 1982, Patuxent reported an average daily population of 687, 47 over the design capacity (Patuxent Institution 1982, 18).

Many at Patuxent did not hail this compromise as a victory. Many clinicians felt at one extreme that Dr. Gluckstern had sold the Institution out, or at a lesser extreme that the treatment program had been severely compromised. Dr. Carney and other clinicians pointed to the continuing erosion of Patuxent's autonomy that began in the early 1970s. Over time, however, some of these same critics came to respect Dr. Gluckstern for her political savvy, and even to admit that the treatment program had not suffered as much as they feared it might. The events that took place from 1988 to 1991 at Patuxent made the Gluckstern compromise seem like a minor incident in the history of the Institution. At the time, though, Dr. Gluckstern may have saved the treatment program from certain disaster.

Following the 1982 issue, Patuxent existed much as it had since 1977—fielding criticism from legislators and the public and fighting for its share of resources. There was still no violence to speak of (though the beating of one inmate by another with an aluminum baseball bat made a significant ripple in the press), and treatment still continued much as it had since 1955. Some changes took place in the diagnostic process (Dr. Carney instituted a pre-screening process to "weed out" the obvious Non-Eligible Persons before too much staff time was spent on them). A research office was created (and directed by this author) which, for the first time since 1955, provided the administration and clinical staff with regular statistics on diagnostics, treatment, inmate characteristics, and recidivism. A legal counsel position was created as another aid to the Director. The parole process underwent a significant change in 1983 when, as the outcome of lobbying from victims' rights advocates, the Maryland legislature passed a bill requiring that the Governor review all parole recommendations for inmates serving life sentences. This change, coupled with a creeping conservatism on the part of the Board of Review, resulted in a logjam of lifers at Patuxent. Eventually, a section of Patuxent was remodeled to accommodate the expanding work release population.[14] In 1988, a combination of events at the national and local levels again focused attention on Patuxent, raised public and legislative criticisms to a high pitch, and brought about perhaps the most dramatic changes to the Patuxent treatment program.

Synopsis

The new era for Patuxent, which began in 1977 and lasted until 1988, marked a significant change for the organization in several significant respects — leadership, administration, and the population of inmates under treatment. We observe, however, that treatment continued much as it had in decades past (individual and group therapy led by trained clinicians, integration with educational and vocational programs, unit treatment teams, graded tier system, release to the community through a graduated, monitored process). We observe also that, while violence and tension within Patuxent lessened considerably, bringing about a decade of relative calm, controversy and criticism of Patuxent continued. The victim's rights movement focused criticism on Patuxent and on parole and release practices generally, bringing about new legislation that affected Patuxent's ability to grant parole. Conservative, anti-Patuxent legislators continued to propose bills to close the Institution.

The Contract Research Corporation (CRC) evaluation study of Patuxent could have been damning. It found no special benefit to the treatment program and questioned the value of the medical model. Were it not, once again, for a small group of activists in government (in this case, a legislative aide working for Governor Mandel along with several key Patuxent supporters) who took it upon themselves to challenge the CRC report and point out that the report's recommendations flew in the face of reforms regarding the treatment of violent criminals that Governor Mandel would soon propose, the legislature might have seized on the CRC report and enacted legislation to close Patuxent.

It is important to note here that just as was the case at the time of Patuxent's creation, at the very point in time that the CRC research was in process, another commission was studying the problem of the violent criminal offender and developing recommendations for legislative change. The compromise worked out between these two initiatives resulted in the revised Article 31-B that retained Patuxent Institution as a treatment prison, albeit with a different admissions procedure that eventually produced a different profile of the offender in treatment (more violent, but less criminal).

Notes

1. It was listed as 509 in another section of the same report.

2. In response to the critics of the old Patuxent, Dr. Francis Carney points out that all inmates confined at Patuxent under the Defective Delinquent law were given the choice to stay and receive treatment under the new law or return to the Division of Correction. Eighty percent of the inmates chose to remain, and a very small number (33) were released outright because their original sentence had expired. Some years later a follow-up of the 33 inmates was conducted, which revealed that 23 of them were convicted for new criminal offenses.

3. This number, $16,000, differs from the reported per capita figure for Patuxent in Fiscal Year 1986 of $21,020. In Fiscal Year 1984 the Maryland Department of Public Safety changed the formula for calculating per capita cost for all Maryland correctional institutions. The FY 1986 figure was adjusted to make it comparable to the FY 1978 figure.

4. Much of this material is gleaned from the manuscript of Dr. Francis Carney, former Chief Psychologist at Patuxent and an employee there from 1969 to 1989. Interviews with former employees, staff of the Governor's office, and other criminal justice professionals also contributed to this section.

5. Recall that an earlier case, the *Sas* case, had called for a thorough review of Patuxent's constitutionality. *Tippett* came about as a result of *Sas*.

6. As Dr. Carney relates the story, one of the men under his treatment had taken the officer hostage and beaten him, after which some other inmates joined in the "mini-revolt."

7. Dr. Carney relates that, because the defendants in the class action suit included a group of violent, black militants who called themselves "The Patuxent Thirteen," holding the hearings at Patuxent avoided the risk of transporting the inmates to and from a court each day.

8. Wilner had accompanied Governor Mandel on some of his trips to Patuxent to quell various disturbances.

9. At the time he received a copy of the CRC report, Alan Wilner's commission had completed its work. He had turned his attention to his regular duties as Chief Legislative Officer, which meant he was busy promoting Governor Mandel's interests in the legislature.

10. These data are from administrative records. They do not reflect randomly drawn populations. The differences are instructive, however. The issue of racial representation in the Patuxent population is an issue that has always lurked in the background. Some observers claim Patuxent was created by white, Jewish legislators as a safe haven for white criminals, while others have claimed it to be another part of a criminal justice system prejudiced against blacks. Unfortunately, these sensitive questions have never been researched adequately.

11. Recall that the Secretariat system was not instituted in Maryland government until 1970, fifteen years after Patuxent was founded.

12. The 1982 Annual Report for Patuxent Institution listed a design capacity of 640 (which is assumed to apply to the previous year since no significant construction took place), and a "therapeutic" capacity of 610. The clinicians and the Patuxent administration have always argued that a treatment system that relies on a graded tier system must always maintain a certain portion of

empty cells. Inmate control, and the rewarding and punishment system, depends on empty beds at all levels, otherwise movement based on behavior cannot take place.

13. The CRC study showed the Maryland Institution for Women (MCIW) cost more to operate than other state correctional institutions (CRC, 1977, 140), but MCIW costs were rarely used to compare with Patuxent.

14. In 1982, 21% of the Eligible Person population was serving a life sentence (n=106). In 1986, the percentage had dropped to 19% (n=88). Data were not available for the number of inmates on parole or work release status with life sentences.

Chapter Eight

The Second Rebirth: The 1988 Presidential Election and Its Impact on Patuxent Institution

Late in the presidential election campaign of 1988, a criminal justice issue emerged to dominate the campaign in its waning months. It became known that Willie Horton, an inmate and first-degree murderer, had been furloughed from Massachusetts in 1986 while Michael Dukakis (the presidential candidate of the Democratic Party) was Governor. Willie Horton traveled to Maryland, raped a Maryland woman and savagely beat her fiancé in 1987, a crime for which he was caught and punished. In October 1988, the Maryland Republican Party ran a television add criticizing Governor Dukakis for being weak on crime control. The ad showed a picture of Dukakis superimposed next to Willie Horton. The Democratic party became incensed over this bit of negative campaigning, from which the George Bush (Republican) campaign committee divorced itself. Soon thereafter, the Maryland Democratic party released to the press a copy of a Republican fund-raising letter it had obtained. The letter pictured Dukakis with Willie Horton, with the following headline, "Is this your pro-family team for 1988?" (*The Washington Post*, December 6, 1988, D7). Elections analysts decried the negative campaigning, but agreed that it was effective in placing Dukakis on the defensive, and that the strategy hurt his campaign. George Bush won the election, but the battle was just shaping up for Patuxent.

Conflict over Release Practices

The campaign issue raised concern across the country about furlough programs, and brought this particular criminal justice issue into the forefront. In November 1988, the news broke that Patuxent had been granting furloughs to a triple murderer named Robert Daly Angell since April of that year. Angell, who was serving a triple life sentence, had killed two teenagers and a police officer in Montgomery County following a bank robbery in 1976 (*The Washington Post*, November 20, 1988, B1, B5). That same newspaper article made reference to Fernando Stewart, who had killed a police officer in 1973, who was on parole from Patuxent and about whom Patuxent refused to provide any information, citing rules of confidentiality.

Two days later it was reported in the *Post* that Angell's Thanksgiving furlough was canceled after it had been approved, that all Thanksgiving furloughs from Patuxent would be suspended, and that the Board of Review would meet in early December to consider the Christmas furloughs. Secretary Robinson was quoted as saying he planned to review the Board's furlough policy. It was reported that Governor Schaffer had ordered an investigation of the furlough program by his staff, and that Senator Denis (Republican, Montgomery County) planned to introduce a bill that would deny furloughs to certain violent offenders (*The Washington Post*, November 22, 1988, A1, A12).

Editorials began to appear on corrections and rehabilitation, all of which referred to these developments at Patuxent. On November 29, 1988, the *Post* printed a story about a Maryland woman who was planning to move away from Maryland because in 1987 Patuxent had recommended parole to Clarence Hancock, who had killed her sister brutally in 1976. Governor Schaffer had denied the parole, but it became evident that Hancock was on work release status at Patuxent. At the same time, Roberta Roper, who headed the influential Roper Commission and was a leading victims' rights advocate in the state, was quoted as saying that closing Patuxent would be too drastic a measure, but that she did not feel society had an obligation to rehabilitate capital murderers, even if it is possible (*The Washington Post*, November 29, 1988, B1, B7).[1]

Up to this point, many viewed criticism of Patuxent a result of the aftermath of the presidential campaign. While Patuxent's practices could be found wanting, no information appeared which linked any Patuxent releasees to any violent criminal behavior. Patuxent and state officials were concentrating more on damage control in the wake of the Willie Horton issue, than on evidence that Patuxent was a failure.

Patuxent Parolee Absconds, Conflict Intensifies

On November 28, 1988, James Stavarakas, a convicted rapist on work release from Patuxent, absconded from the program. The next day, a woman was raped close to the spot where Stavarakas committed the rape he had been sentenced for in 1976. The victim's description of the rapist matched that of Stavarakas, and the Maryland State Police mentioned him as a suspect. Dr. Gluckstern immediately suspended the work release program, reviewed the inmates on work release at the time, and reinstated the program on a limited basis (*The Washington Post*, November 30, 1988, D1, D5). The same article reported that the Montgomery County Police Association was requesting that a 1987 law barring Patuxent from admitting inmates with multiple life sentences, be applied to Robert Angell. If the court ruled in their favor, he would be removed from Patuxent and no longer eligible for work release under the Patuxent program. Angell's admission to Patuxent predated the law, and the writer doubted the court would find in the Association's favor.

Stavarakas surrendered to authorities in North Carolina early in December 1988. It became known that just before he absconded from work release, the Patuxent Board of Review had revoked his parole after a urine sample had tested positive for controlled substances. He was placed on work release following the revocation of parole. Dr. Gluckstern reported that the work release program would be suspended until the Secretary's office conducted a thorough review, and criticism of Patuxent increased from the Governor's staff and the legislature (*The Washington Post*, December 5, 1988, A1, A4).

The Maryland legislature convened after the holidays in January 1989, and quickly took up the Patuxent controversy. A special legislative committee recommended changes at Patuxent Institution such as limiting the Institution's paroling authority, restricting its ability to admit violent murderers and sex offenders, requiring that such violent offenders serve the minimum criminal sentence before being considered for parole, and restructuring the Board of Review so that the appointed citizen members, not the Patuxent administration, have the majority of votes. Secretary Robinson was reported as supporting these changes and of reducing the Institution's autonomy greatly (*The Washington Post*, January 10, 1989, front page, A10, D3).

In mid-January 1989, Dr. Gluckstern took an extended medical leave from Patuxent Institution. She was quoted as saying Secretary Robinson had not forced her to leave. Several legislators criticized her, and one doubted she would return (*The Washington Post*, January 26, 1989, B3). She never returned.

Legislative Restructuring

In February 1989, the Maryland House of Delegates approved legislation to restructure the practices at Patuxent Institution; the vote passed 126–0. The changes included:

- All Board of Review decisions are subject to the review of the Secretary of Public Safety and Correctional Services.

- The Board of Review was reconstituted into the Citizen Review Board to include the Director of Patuxent, the three Associate Directors, and five members to be appointed by the Governor, including one representative from a victims' rights group. A "supermajority" of at least seven of the nine votes is required to approve release on parole recommendations.

- Any inmate who violates certain parole provisions (committing a crime, using drugs, and several others) will be expelled from Patuxent.

- First degree murderers and rapists are barred from admission to Patuxent, unless the sentencing judge recommends it; and those with life sentences cannot be released until they have served as much of their criminal sentences as they would in other state prisons.

Secretary Robinson was charged with writing new policies for Patuxent that would put these changes into effect (*The Washington Post*, February 15, 1989, B1–B5; February 23, 1989, A1, A16).

In December 1989, following a competitive review process, the second major evaluation of Patuxent Institution was awarded to Abt Associates, Inc., in Massachusetts. Abt reported the following findings to the Maryland Department of Public Safety and Correctional Services in December 1990:

> We find no evidence of any effect of Patuxent treatment on subsequent recidivism, as measured by the probability of being arrested following release to supervision. More precisely, we find no evidence that being confined at Patuxent contributes to lower recidivism rates, compared to spending one's sentence partly or entirely within the Division of Correction's prisons. Nor do we find evidence that Patuxent releasees do worse from the point of view of subsequent arrests. (McDonald et al. 1990, 67)

There were other, similarly damning, findings. Curiously, the final report received little press coverage and little attention at the legislature in Annapolis.

Following Dr. Gluckstern's retirement, Secretary Robinson appointed a new Director of Patuxent, Joseph Henneberry. Mr. Henneberry had been an administrator at St. Elizabeth's Hospital in Washington, D.C., the District's hospital for the criminally insane. He set in motion the necessary activities to re-write Patuxent's rules and regulations to accommodate the new version of Article 31-B. These were released for public comment in February 1990, and approved soon thereafter.

As the public furor died down, the aftermath of these developments was felt at Patuxent. Much as had occurred when Dr. Gluckstern first became Director, one-by-one the Associate Directors resigned; many other staff left as well. Early in 1991, the Institution population exceeded 1,100, while the design capacity had not changed from 640. An inmate committed suicide. The new Citizen Review Board was appointed, with Arthur Marshall as its Chair. Mr. Marshall was a former State's Attorney from Prince George's County, Maryland. During his tenure in office, he was one of the most outspoken critics of Patuxent and an advocate for victims' rights. The parole and release programs were almost at a standstill.

Another development was taking place nationally that was to have an indirect impact on Patuxent, and that may have saved the treatment program from total elimination. The mid- to late 1980s witnessed the nation's "war on drugs." The U.S. Congress and the Office of the President, while they often clashed over tactics, supported the war on drugs with funding initiatives and a state and local assistance program that bears close resemblance to the Law Enforcement Assistance Administration of the 1970s.[2] Two developments took place nationally that are of interest to this analysis:

1. The increased attention, and the increased resources, brought to drug problems and drug crime as a result of the war on drugs caused prison populations to increase nationwide. Nearly every state experienced an increase in admissions to prison for drug offenses, and an increase in the percentage contribution of drug offenders to the prison population.

2. Interest in drug treatment increased, as did resources devoted to research in that area. Many states revisited the debate about coercion to treatment (for drug offenders). Interest, debate, and information about treatment issues in corrections increased as a result of the war on drugs.

Under Dr. Henneberry's tenure, Patuxent Institution applied for, and received, from the National Institute of Corrections a small grant to implement a drug treatment program. Conversations with Director Henneberry and other Patuxent staff suggest that Patuxent would still be treating inmates using a group therapy, graded tier, integrated approach. The types of inmates under treatment would likely change, and the parole and release process was sure to change dramatically.

The regulations drafted to accommodate changes to Article 31-B list the following under a section called "Special Populations Criteria:"

> A. The Division [of Correction] shall give special consideration to the referral of inmates specified in Regulation .01 ['General Referral Criteria'], and who also meet one or more of the following special population criteria:
>
> (1) Chronically mentally disordered;
>
> (2) Chronic youthful offenders who meet the criteria of Courts and Judicial Proceedings Article, Para. 3-804(e), Annotated Code of Maryland; or

(3) Mentally retarded (Maryland Register, Friday, February 23, 1990).

As was noted above, under the new rules most Citizen Review Board decisions would be subject to the review of the Secretary of Public Safety and Correctional Services. In effect, much of Patuxent's autonomy was removed. Administrative and clinical staff control over admissions was diminished, and almost entirely removed from the release decision. The treatment work that clinicians performed, however—group therapy, including the therapy modality, monitoring of progress in therapy, development of the treatment plan, makeup of therapy groups, and many other practices—remained untouched. While the pool of inmates available for treatment changed, it was still chiefly the clinical staff that formulated the treatment program and that recommended inmates for release on leaves, work release or parole. They found themselves working with a much more conservative and less clinically oriented Board, however.

Most significant, perhaps, is that treatment was still included in the Institution's mission statement and legislative mandate. The term "rehabilitation," however, was replaced by the more politically palatable: "remediation." Without the protection of a legal mandate, Patuxent might lose its mission entirely and become subsumed, if not officially, in practice, under the Division of Correction. When asked why Patuxent has such staying power in the face of such criticism and conservative philosophy about corrections, Delegate Pauline Menes, a member of the Maryland General Assembly since 1966 and respected for her involvement in correctional issues, stated the following:

> Just...I don't know. There is a small cadre of people who believe in redemption and re-education, and the ability of human beings with a spark of life and a desire to live free, to change behavior. With few exceptions, we do not give up on people...And I think there is a spark in every state administrator, be it Commissioner or the Secretary, who the spark says to them, "Could you be spending your life doing a job where you have no hope of really making anything happen, and really improving the chances of stopping criminal activity?" Patuxent is that little voice that says to them, "Keep at it. We may be finding an answer here."...Without Patuxent, there's

> really nothing that one can look to and that must be very depressing and very discouraging. (Interview with Pauline Menes, 1/19/90)

Synopsis

This most recent legitimacy crisis for Patuxent Institution had as its catalyst, again, several serious criminal acts (this time by offenders on release in Maryland or specifically from Patuxent) that factored in a national presidential election campaign. Again, we observe a special study, legislative inquiry and debate, and eventually legislative action affecting Patuxent directly, but not abolishing the Institution. Curiously, in this instance, the study finding "no effect" from clinical treatment at Patuxent (inmates treated at Patuxent, according to the study, performed no better or worse than those confined in the regular Division of Correction) received little public or press attention, and it had minimal impact on the debates and negotiations surrounding Patuxent's future.

In this legitimacy crisis, the focus is on community release (work release and parole) decisions, and the authority to make them, rather than on specific clinical treatment practices at Patuxent. At the conclusion of this sequence of events, Patuxent remains intact, however, with significant curtailment of its (staff's) authority to release treated offenders back to the community. New rules governing Patuxent changed the composition of the Board of Review (now called the Citizen Review Board), and new admissions criteria precluded certain serious offenders from obtaining treatment at Patuxent. While the treatment program and orientation at Patuxent was not directly threatened during this particular legitimacy crisis, it is likely that these changes in admissions and release criteria will have an impact (as yet unknown) on the clinical treatment practices at Patuxent.

Notes

1. Roper's comments were presumably in response to the following quote from Dr. Gluckstern, which appeared in the same article:

> ...[the Institution] may not have been as sensitive in the past few years to public perception...The [citizens] have to make the decision about whether an inmate or anybody has the right to a second chance...If they feel that there are people who should never be released from prison until their time is served, then that legislation needs to be passed...I think that [our policies] can be adjusted at this point without wiping out the Institution.

2. LEAA, as the program was called, created a state formula funding program, and a concomitant bureaucratic structure, for the purposes of improving crime control and developing coordinated reporting on crime and the criminal justice systems from state and local levels to the federal level. Often criticized as an unnecessary and expensive layer of bureaucracy, the program was dismantled by Attorney General Griffin Bell under the Carter administration. The Anti Drug-Abuse Acts of 1986 and 1988 created a state and local assistance program for drug crime control under the control of the U.S. Department of Justice, Bureau of Justice Assistance (BJA). BJA administers a state formula grant program much like the one created by LEAA.

Chapter Nine

Summary and Conclusions

Public organizations, especially those operating in highly charged public arenas such as correctional rehabilitation, constantly manage and react to contingencies in their immediate and broader environments. As Pfeffer and Salancik (1978) and others in the resource dependency camp suggest, organizational adaptation and survival is the outcome of emergent processes of negotiation and exchange between an organization (and organizational actors) and its immediate (task) as well as its broader environment. As Powell and DiMaggio (1991) and those in the neo-institutionalism camp suggest, organizational adaptation and survival is often the product of larger social and institutional forces (like, in the case of Patuxent, the civil rights movement). In any event, adaptation and survival is an immediate and constant concern for many public organizations. It is at once the product of the deliberate actions of organization actors (either pro-actively or in response to internal and external contingentcies), of organization-environment interactions and exchanges, *and* the product of broad social forces. Organizational theory and research helps sort these phenomena out at different levels of social action. When we apply them to a case study such as this, organizational action is more clearly described and analyzed, and easier to understand. In this chapter we re-examine the key legitimacy and survival challenges faced by Patuxent Institution over its 45-year history in the light of organizational theory, emerging with a sociologically informed understanding of how and why Patuxent has survived as one of the most controversial prisons in America.

Previous chapters described three legitimacy crises for Patuxent Institution that posed threats to the Institution's treatment mission or to its very existence. Two crises—the events leading up to the abolishment of the Defective Delinquent statute in 1975–1977, and the events surrounding the 1988 presidential election—constituted serious threats to Patuxent. They were legitimacy crises that threatened the existence of the prison as a treatment-providing correctional institution. The third crisis—the conflict over resources during a corrections crowding crisis in Maryland in the early 1980s—should not be considered as serious a threat to the Institution's survival as the other crises were. It was a threat nonetheless, since the Secretary of Public Safety was considering stripping Patuxent of its autonomous status and placing it under the administrative authority of the state Division of Correction as a cost saving measure. This move would likely have extended double-celling throughout Patuxent and relegated treatment, if it was attempted at all, to a negligible role.

The analysis traced the events leading up to each crisis, at national, state, and local levels; determined the actors and coalitions that supported and opposed the Institution's treatment mission during each crisis; and described the decisions and sequences of events through the resolution of each crisis. Table 4 below summarizes the events and actors for and against Patuxent for each of the three legitimacy crises.

Table 4
Summary of Events and Actors in Patuxent's History

Dates	Pro-Patuxent	Event	Anti-Patuxent
		Conflict over the Defective Delinquent Statute	
1955–1960	• Correctional Psychiatrists • State Legislators from Baltimore • Governor's Aide	Tension develops between Patuxent and the Maryland Board of Corrections	• Commissioner of Corrections • Inmates Filing Suits vs. Patuxent • State Budget Authority

Continued on next page

Table 4 continued

1960–1977	• Maryland State's Attorney's Office • Maryland Appellate Courts • Noted Psychiatrists • Secretary of Public Safety	Continuing legal challenges to Patuxent	• Inmates Filing Suits vs. Patuxent • County Courts in Maryland • Public Defender's Office
1960–1977	• Legislators from Baltimore • Advisory Boards • Secretary of Public Safety	Anti-Patuxent sentiment in the Maryland legislature and in the press	• Legislators from various counties • *Baltimore Sun* and *Baltimore News American* newspapers • Marylanders vs. Patuxent • College Student Coalitions
1970–1975	• Governor's Office • Advisory Boards • Secretary of Public Safety	Mounting unrest and violence within the prison walls	• Inmate "Refusers" • Radical African American inmates • Civil Rights Movement • Organized Citizens and Advocacy Groups
1975–1976	• Governor's Chief Legislative Officer • Advisory Boards • Court Psychiatrists • Secretary of Public Safety	Legislative action is undertaken; official investigation into Patuxent mandated by the legislature	• Legislators from various counties • Citizens and Citizen Coalitions

continued on next page

Table 4 continued

Conflict over Resources			
1982	• Patuxent administration • Advisory Boards • Various legislators	Maryland correctional facilities crowded; Secretary of Public Safety plans to place Patuxent under the authority of the Division of Correction; Director of Patuxent negotiates to have one building double-celled	• Secretary of Public Safety • Commissioner of Corrections • Various legislators
The 1988 Presidential Election and Patuxent Institution			
Nov. 1988	• Patuxent administration	Press reveals that Patuxent furloughed Robert Angell, a triple murderer and cop killer	• Montgomery county legislators
Nov. 1988	• Patuxent administration • Secretary of Public Safety and Governor (they call for investigations of the furlough program, but do not denounce it)	Press prints further details of the Angell case; prints story of another furloughed inmate	• Citizens and Citizen Coalitions
Nov.–Dec. 1988	• Patuxent administration • Advisory boards • A few legislators	Patuxent work release inmate Stavarakas absconds and is listed as a rape suspect (he later turns himself in)	• Various legislators

continued on next page

Table 4 continued

Jan.–Feb. 1989	• Patuxent administration • Advisory boards • A few legislators	Maryland legislature convenes; special committee recommends changes at Patuxent, including curtailment of paroling authority; changes approved; Director of Patuxent, Dr. Norma Gluckstern, begins extended medical leave and eventually retires	• Maryland legislators • Secretary of Public Safety
Dec. 1990	• A few legislators • Advisory boards	Patuxent evaluation report delivered to Maryland legislature by private contractor; study reports limited effectiveness of Patuxent treatment programs	• Various legislators • Prominent criminal justice professionals

Most of the coalitions or actors that became involved in any of the three crises covered by this research exist at the organization or institution level of responsibility and control (See Table 1, page 43). Each crisis involved actors or groups of actors from Patuxent, advisory boards affiliated with Patuxent, the Maryland legislature, the Maryland Governor's office, state or national professional associations, citizen coalitions, state or county courts, and other organizations that serve institutional-level functions. This finding has two implications for our understanding of Patuxent's survival:

1. Individual actors at the technical (organizational line staff) level rarely play significant roles in the legitimacy crises that

face Patuxent Institution. This is to be expected, since the crises studied were, by definition, crises of the organization, but it is significant for another reason. Powerful individuals at technical and managerial levels, while influential within their spheres of control inside Patuxent Institution, often exert little influence in events and issues from the Institution's environment that threaten the treatment mission.

2. Specific exchanges of power or other institutional resources (tangible or intangible) are difficult to observe, measure, and associate a particular role in any specific legitimacy crisis. The legitimacy crises facing Patuxent are played out in super-organization contexts—in the legislature, in the courts, in the press, for example. Thus, the outcomes of specific crises and the actions taken by pro-Patuxent or anti-Patuxent actors or coalitions will not fit into an equation that compares actions and power on one side to actions and power on the other, with the result being the difference. The outcomes of Patuxent-environment legitimacy crises must be interpreted from an analysis of institutional-level influences as well as organization-environment interactions.

How Patuxent Adapts

Formal and informal adaptive processes operate in Patuxent Institution's adaptation to its external environment, and adaptive processes take place primarily at organizational and institutional levels. An explanation of these processes provides the sociological interpretation of how Patuxent Institution interacts with its task environment to maintain its legitimacy and, in effect, to survive in its charged political environment.

The distinction offered here between formal and informal processes at work in the adaptation of Patuxent Institution to its environment is instructive, but not meant to suggest that there is such a clear distinction in the everyday world of organizational survival. Formal processes have informal components, and both are often at work at the same time. Put another way, informal processes often take place in the context of more formal ones. A complete explanation of one must include an explanation of the other. Nonetheless, the formal and informal characteristics of adaptive processes are important to differentiate in such explanations because these different characteristics point to different sociological, political, and social psychological processes, which must be accounted for in theory development.

Formal Processes

This research revealed several formal processes that work to insure the survival of Patuxent Institution as a treatment-providing correctional institution, in the face of strong social and political forces that work against it. The five processes are described below.

Legal Culture and Precedent. Nationally and in the State of Maryland there has been a history of defective delinquent-type statutes (statutes that define particular classes of violent and/or mentally or socially deficient offenders, and provide for special criminal justice processing or treatment for them).[1] While few exist today, the notion is not foreign to those familiar with psychiatry and the law. Additionally, Article 31-B has been on the books for over 30 years in Maryland. It is more difficult to repeal a law creating a state agency than it is to rescind an administrative directive such as an executive order or memorandum of agreement. It is even more difficult to repeal a law after it has been on the books for such a long period of time, even if it has been the center of much controversy. Thus, precedent plays a role in the adaptation and survival of Patuxent

Institution, as do the existing national and local legal cultures that recognize the possibility, validity, and viability of "defective delinquent" or other special offender categories.

Organizational Adaptation through the Legislative Process. The process of creating and amending Patuxent's enabling legislation (in this case, at the state level, but the case can be made for other levels of government) is, in and of itself, an adaptive process for a public organization. The legislative process, from initial bill drafting and debate, and through subsequent debate and revision, is a very formal one. In the context of state politics, public safety and provision of correctional services, Patuxent's legitimacy, budget, authorization, mandate, regulations, staffing levels, and outcomes (successes and failures) are matters of legislative debate and record. These formal processes have been perhaps the most visible in the history of Patuxent, and it has been through them that Article 31-B has been officially drafted and revised over the years. It is important to note two issues regarding this formal adaptive process:

1. Adaptation does not equal organizational survival. Patuxent Institution still exists as a treatment-providing prison, and the delivery of treatment services (clinical therapy) takes place today in much the same way that it did in the past; but it is not the same organization. The state has curtailed its autonomy to the point where it no longer has final say in its release decisions, and admissions practices have been similarly constrained. Its resources have been stretched to the point where provision of clinical services is constrained financially. While treatment is provided according to the medical model (see Epilogue for clarification on this point), the less clinical and more administrative (but no less important) components of the treatment process have been altered to such a degree as to constrain the treatment process.

2. Adaptation is a reactive process, and Patuxent's history is a reflection of such processes. As a public organization with little raw power, Patuxent Institution reacts to the legislative and political processes that surround it, rather than forcefully pushing its interests in political circles and at the legislature.

State Bureaucracy and Conflict Resolution. The formal administrative structure of public safety, law enforcement, and criminal justice in Maryland acts as a venue for adaptive processes in a manner similar to the legislative process discussed above. The bureaucratic procedures that exist to transfer information and ideas between Patuxent and its primary organizational counterparts (other state prisons, other state criminal justice agencies) and superiors (the Secretary's office, the Board of Patuxent) provide filters and buffers which help the Patuxent administration interact with members from more hostile components of the task environment (the legislature, the press, advocacy groups, the judiciary). In this manner conflicts and potential threats to legitimacy are worked out in the normal course of business, a buffer against the development of more serious and potentially damaging conflicts.

Adaptive Processes in the Task Environment. As a semi-independent organization, Patuxent does not adapt to constraints in its task environment (the set of organizations and actors in its immediate periphery that it must work with to perform its own functions and responsibilities) in the sense that the organization interacts with component organizations and actors in the task environment. More accurately, Patuxent Institution reacts to adaptive processes that take place in its task environment. For example, the change in Article 31-B from "defective delinquent, indeterminate sentence" statute to "eligible person, determinate sentence" statute was the result of formal and informal exchanges and maneuvering between the

Governor's office and the legislature. There were many incidents involving Patuxent leading up to the change in the law, but the posturing, negotiating, drafting of new legislation, and debate over studies of Patuxent did not occur much between Patuxent and elements of its environment; they took place primarily between the Secretary's office, the Governor's office, the legislature, and other interested or politically active parties. By the time the actual negotiating took place, the Patuxent administration was ineffective, relegated to such status by the long series of incidents and bad press that preceded the change in the law.

The same can be said of the most recent change in Article 31-B. By the time the legislature acted to revise Article 31-B in 1989, Patuxent was powerless to do anything but wait and watch the legislative and political processes taking place in the legislature and at the Secretary's office.

The same cannot be said of the conflict over resources in 1982, when Patuxent's Director agreed to double-cell Division of Correction inmates to avoid a more heated battle in the legislature. When Dr. Gluckstern acted to ward off the larger conflict, she demonstrated political savvy and power in her capacity as the organization's executive.

Thus, the "action," or the adaptive processes that shape Patuxent, takes place more often outside the institution in the task environment than between Patuxent and its task environment. Patuxent merely reacts to the outcomes of conflicts in its environment.

Adaptation through Organization Management. While Patuxent's environment stands out as the principal determinant of survival for the organization, there are formal processes and mechanisms that originate within the organization in the vein of classical organization theory. There are examples of coalescing, co-opting, and boundary spanning (from Thompson, 1967) to be found at Patuxent, developed specifically by organization management to protect the Institution from elements in its environment. For example, Patuxent's two chief administrative aides that report to the Director (the legal officer[2] and research director) perform important boundary spanning activities. The legal officer monitors each legislative session to spot proposed bills early that will affect Patuxent, to give the Director lead time in fashioning testimony and organization responses to the proposed legislation.[3] The research director monitors administrative activities at the organization's boundaries (e.g., referrals to Patuxent, admissions, releases), national and other research on treatment and correctional issues, as well as organizational practices that may provoke reactions from elements in the environment (e.g., parole practices, revocations and recidivism, costs).

Patuxent administrators have initiated co-opting (absorbing new, and potentially conflicting, elements into the organizational leadership) and coalescing (when organizations with little power seek joint ventures with other organizations in the task environment) strategies to help ensure organization survival. For example, around 1985 a prominent physician at Johns Hopkins University who was gaining national recognition for his treatment of sex offenders using group therapy and chemical therapy (depo provera, a testosterone reducing drug) visited Patuxent to talk with clinical staff about his work. A number of ex-Patuxent inmates (who had been re-arrested and returned to the Division of Correction) were under his care. During his visits to Patuxent he was openly (but constructively) critical of Patuxent's clinical practices, which resulted in, predictably, mixed reactions on the part of Patuxent staff. Shortly thereafter he was appointed to the Board of Patuxent. The criticisms did not stop, but they were kept more within the confines of Board deliberations.

Most recently, examples of coalescing are evident in Patuxent Institution Annual Reports and newly devised administrative regulations to cast Patuxent Institution as a "partner" of sorts with the Division of Correction. Prominence is given to the fact that Patuxent is helping ease the Division's crowding problems by exceeding its rated capacity, as well as to the fact that Patuxent exists to provide services to Division of Correction inmates.

Another example of competitive strategies initiated by Patuxent is found in "prestige seeking." As many public organizations do, Patuxent attempts to manage its prestige, status, and legitimacy in the task environment by creating a positive image or by reducing negative images of the organization. Twice during her tenure as Director, Dr. Gluckstern held public and research conferences within the prison grounds, with the aim of reducing the myths and negative images held by public officials about Patuxent and, in the case of a national corrections research conference held in 1988, generating positive images about the Institution among correctional administrators and researchers. Dr. Boslow and his colleagues made similar attempts in earlier years, by publishing in correctional journals and participating in such organizations as the Association of Correctional Psychologists.

Informal Processes

Two informal processes that work to ensure Patuxent's survival as an organization emerged from this research. One is directly and inextricably linked to some of the more formal processes described above; and the other is related to the tendency for organizations to provide informal mechanisms for avoiding their own formal processes.

Adaptation through the Informal Workings of Political Coalitions. There are a number of coalitions (alliances of groups or individuals) that have operated in informal manners as key components of adaptive processes between Patuxent and its environment. They are composed of individuals from distinct professions (e.g., lawyers, psychiatrists, judges, legislators, members of Patuxent's various boards), though individuals from any of these professions may participate in coalitions for or against Patuxent. For example, there were legislators supportive of Patuxent, and those that tried to close it down. Generally, the anti-Patuxent coalitions were more formally organized (in the sense that they consciously united, or met frequently, to organize their anti-Patuxent activities—demonstrations, testimony, lobbying, backing anti-Patuxent legislation). There are few examples of organized pro-Patuxent coalitions. Pro-Patuxent coalitions were groups of individuals that were already organized for other purposes (for example, Patuxent clinicians, Patuxent board members, members of legislative committees), but they did not organize for the purpose of supporting Patuxent or drafting strategies to do so. Following (Table 5) are examples of the key pro- and anti-Patuxent coalitions that operated in adaptation processes.

There were formal mechanisms for these coalitions to participate in adaptive processes, such as the legislative process, the courts, and other forums for public and political debate and action. At the same time, though, these coalitions worked in informal manners to achieve the same objectives being pursued by formal means. For example, the 1977 version of Article 31-B was submitted to the legislature as a "governor's bill," a bill drafted by Governor Marvin Mandel's staff as a legislative initiative from the executive branch of state government; and formal debate and voting ensued. At the same time, the Governor's staff and other Patuxent supporters worked in informal, or less formal, ways to promote the bill's passage by writing letters, making phone calls, and making personal visits to key legislators to convince them of the value of the legislation, or to discredit the efforts of others to oppose the legislation. Members of anti-Patuxent coalitions pursued the same informal means. These informal processes go hand-in-hand with the formal legal and political processes described above and, as others have argued, seem to be critical components of organizational adaptation processes. This is especially the case with public organizations, whose success depends more on the status of their legitimacy rather than on their material or tangible products.

Table 5
Key Political Coalitions in Patuxent's Environment

Pro-Patuxent	Anti-Patuxent
Members of the Baltimore Judiciary	Members of the Judiciary from Montgomery and Prince George's Counties
Legislators from Baltimore and Prince George's County	Legislators from Montgomery and other Maryland Counties
Most Maryland Governors	The Baltimore Press
Most Secretaries of Public Safety and Correctional Services	Citizen Advocacy Groups (ACLU, Marylanders Against Patuxent, Roper Committee)

Informal Processes as Escape Valves for Systemic Failures. A number of respondents from inside Patuxent and from its task environment voiced the following argument during the course of this research: Patuxent exists because the Maryland criminal justice system (the judiciary in particular) needed an escape hatch through which certain offenders could avoid the traditional (hard core) prison system.[4] Whatever the motivation of those who recommended confinement at Patuxent, the notion of Patuxent as an escape valve is illuminating. Many pro-Patuxent individuals or coalitions doubted the ability of traditional prisons to rehabilitate offenders, or at least felt the need for an alternative to traditional incarceration for certain types of offenders. It is conceivable, then, that for various reasons Patuxent came into being, and survived its many tumultuous years, because key coalitions wanted to keep the escape valve open. From this perspective, Patuxent exists partially as the result of informal (or hidden) processes operating to circumvent the formal (punishment-oriented) correctional system in Maryland.

These formal and informal processes provide insight into **how** Patuxent survives in its hostile environment—the actors involved, actions taken, situation-specific elements, roles, and bureaucratic processes that work to support the Institution. They do not answer the question posed at the outset of this research: **Why** does society, which does not generally recognize rehabilitation as a legitimate goal for a prison, allow Patuxent to survive, and to provide treatment based on a medical model often described as outdated and inappropriate? To answer this question, we must turn to the neo-institutional perspective on society and complex organizations, and return to the analytical framework presented in Table 1 (page 43).

The key to understanding why Patuxent survives lies in two phenomena explained by neo-institutional theory. First, Patuxent fulfills a legitimizing function in local and larger society that transcends political and bureaucratic issues of cost effectiveness, recidivism, or utility of the Institution—the concepts debated most frequently and vociferously during legitimacy crises. This legitimizing function is the ideology of treatment. It has its roots in the social and medical sciences and is often linked to the concept of humanitarianism. The ideology of treatment is not as strong, or perhaps not as visible and vocal as it was decades ago, but it remains a precept of many professionals working in corrections (including clinical professionals, social workers, and correctional officers). Patuxent's status as "half prison–half mental hospital" has always made it easier for treatment ideology to work its way into the prison culture there.

Patuxent, it can be argued, has a less ideological and more political function—that of legitimizing the local and statewide correctional system. The existence of Patuxent, an organization that provides treatment to less than 10 percent of the state's incarcerated population (under the legitimizing concept of "Eligible Person") allows politicians to hold up the Institution as a model of humanitarianism, thus steering attention away from the other 90 percent of inmates that may live under more oppressive conditions. Similarly, when things go bad at Patuxent (when inmates on work release commit new crimes, for example), focusing criticism on that Institution provides a shelter for equally bad practices at the state's other correctional facilities.

Second, Patuxent also provides a vehicle for public and political debate over the value of treatment and correctional rehabilitation. It has a dual and conflicting legal mandate—to punish and to treat; an inexact technology—clinical treatment, with few agreed upon processes or measures; and it operates at the whim of a legislature and public that understand little about clinical treatment issues. In such an environment, debates about Patuxent become couched in terms of hope or despair ("at least we're trying something to treat criminals," "if we didn't do what we do at Patuxent, nothing positive would happen anywhere in corrections," "to do away with Patuxent is to give up on these people who are in legitimate need of treatment"). Debates about the legitimacy of Patuxent, while touching on political and bureaucratic issues, really become debates over the treatment-rehabilitation ideal. At the societal or institutional level, it is more difficult to abandon these ideals than at the single organization or local level.

These arguments explain the phenomenon of Patuxent's survival, along with the traditional organizational concepts of bureaucracy and exchange processes described above, better than the traditional arguments regarding organizational management, resource dependency, and other theoretical formulations with a narrower focus on organization-environment interactions. They allow for the existence of a conflict between societal sectors regarding Patuxent, and between societal levels. They mix well with the more traditional, micro-level phenomena explained by this research; and they allow for super-organizational forces to contribute to the explanation of Patuxent's survival.

Synopsis of Findings

As difficult as it may be to summarize the findings of this social and historical analysis of Patuxent Institution covering over 45 years, several general points represent the contribution of this work to organizational research on prisons.

First, we find that there is indeed room for correctional facilities like Patuxent in American corrections, facilities that have the primary purpose of rehabilitating violent or serious offenders with mental health and emotional problems. At the very least, it is possible to operate a maximum-security prison in which custody (safety and security) and treatment (rehabilitation) have equal standing in the organizational culture and operations. This fact seems to be missed by many of our correctional leaders today, who justify their safe, clean, and quiet prisons by sacrificing rehabilitative treatment programs. In addition, the social and political will exists to support the operation of prisons like Patuxent Institution.

Second, such correctional facilities that operate in high risk environments will encounter real legitimacy crises from time to time, and the resolution of those crises often takes place in unusual ways. It seems a fair amount of serendipity and opportunism comes into play. In the case of Patuxent Institution, resolution of several major legitimacy crises required several key factors—supportive legislators, interested and engaged parties in the governor's office, and other interested groups or coalitions. For example, the creation of Patuxent and the resolution of its first legitimacy crises involved negotiations between several commissions that were looking into issues regarding violent criminals. The result of this process produced the solution, not the isolated planning and work of either one alone. In addition, several creative and energetic people helped make these things happen. They saw the developing opportunities and seized upon them to resolve a problem at hand.

Third, we witnessed clearly the role of the courts in policy reform, primarily through case law, and not always with the anticipated outcome. In the case of Patuxent Institution, many legal challenges to its operation were brought to the courts over several decades beginning in 1955 with the opening of the Institution. As we saw, the challengers to Patuxent won some key decisions in the lower courts, most of which were reversed on appeal (sometimes years later). Over the long term, the courts have significant impact on correctional change and reform. No matter what the eventual outcome, the process can be troubling. In the case of Patuxent Institution, early court victories, appeals, and later reversals caused problems for the Institution, and likely contributed to tensions and outbreaks of violence.

Fourth, like other organizations, prisons have life cycles. They are born (created), they have growing pains, they mature, and sometimes they die or, in the case of Patuxent, are reborn in different forms. This organizational life cycle is fascinating. It is influenced by many factors, small and large, local and national, in predictable and unpredictable ways. Because they are public, controversial, and "hidden" organizations, they are less studied than others like schools or hospitals. Still, studying them in this fashion, and learning in depth how they work and why they work the way they do, helps us understand them better, helps us understand our justice system better, and helps us understand ourselves better.

Illumination of Organizational Theory and Research

Conclusions about the formal and informal processes that make up the key components of the adaptation processes that occur between Patuxent and its environment (or simply within the task environment), based on the findings of this case study, have implications for current sociological theories about complex organizations, and about research that needs to take place to further test and elaborate on them. This final section considers these two issues as well as the multi-level approach to organizational research that will be required to further the merging of functionalist and neo-institutionalist perspectives on complex organizations.

This research began with the premise that public organizations are different from private organizations. At the conclusion of this research, this distinction seems to be critical to the future of theory development for public organizations. The distinction between public and private organizations was instructive as a guidepost for this case study, but it has not been developed enough to present clear distinctions between private, semi-private or semi-public, and public organizations. In the case of Patuxent Institution, the organization is so clearly a public entity that few would argue against the use of the distinction. Prisons produce so few tangible products, and fewer products that have value in economic markets, that classifying them as private organizations (even if some of them are managed by private sector corporations) is not appropriate.

Two aspects of prisons in America suggest a reconsideration of such a perspective. First, the debate over privatization of corrections is not over in this country. If privatization of corrections produces cost savings for governments that can be calculated by some agreeable standards, then prisons (or the business of public safety and corrections) will take on more characteristics of private organizations, at least to the extent that private prisons are expected to produce cost savings to governments.[5] Arguably, then, such "private" prisons, regardless of their orientation toward treatment and rehabilitation, will experience fewer and milder legitimacy crises.

Second, prison industries operate in many states. These are business enterprises, operated primarily through state prisons that compete in open (or regulated) markets. Common, though somewhat dated, examples of prison industries include farming (as described in Martin and Eckland-Olson's *Texas Prisons: The Walls Came Tumbling Down)* furniture making, or license plate making operations. A more modern version of prison industries is found in Patuxent's license plate tag printing operation.[6] Prisons that operate profit-making enterprises, or business enterprises in competitive markets, will take on certain characteristics of private organizations. Their success or legitimacy may rest, at least in part, on more traditional private sector measures of efficiency or profit making.

At this point in time, neither privatization nor prison industries has had such an impact on the correctional system to suggest that radical shifts in current ways of evaluating their operations will soon take place.

There are competing theories regarding complex organizations. The classical theorists (Thompson, Barnard, and others) assume significant influence on the part of organization executives; theirs is a management-oriented approach. Mechanisms such as adaptation, cooptation, and boundary spanning take place at the initiative of the organization executive or manager (though limited rationality is understood on their parts). Examples of these adaptive maneuvers were observed at Patuxent, but principally in situations that involved lower-level controversies over resources or particular clinical practices, as opposed to higher-level controversies over the legitimacy of the Institution. Different theories of complex organizations, such as political economy theory (from Wamsley and Zald) or resource dependence theory (from Pfeffer and Salancik) place more control relating to organizational survival in the environment of the organization, rather than in the hands of organization managers and executives. Such theories explain much more of Patuxent's adaptation than do classical theories, and elements of both were observed.

Management of political economy (status, legitimacy, key supporting coalitions, and images of the organization in the environment) is a constant organizational endeavor for Patuxent, but the organization is often limited in the extent to which it can participate in active management of its political economy. In times of intense debate and negative public sentiment about Patuxent, the Secretary's office will take steps to curtail the public activities of the Director. In less controversial times, Patuxent management will engage in positive image building, networking among supportive coalitions, and perhaps even controversial treatment programs, but as soon as the environment creates strong negative sentiment about Patuxent, such activities will lessen considerably, by the choices of Patuxent leadership and mandate from the Secretary's office.

Resource dependency theory helps makes sense of much of the adaptive processes operating in the case of Patuxent Institution. Any power exercised by Patuxent, perceptions of its value or effectiveness, or flexibility in how it conducts its business are so inextricably linked to elements in the organization's task environment as to make it seem that these things are "granted" to the Institution from time to time, rather than earned by the Institution or taken by it in power struggles. The office of the Secretary of Public Safety and Correctional Services, the Maryland legislature (specifically the House Committee on Public Safety and Transportation, which reviews and authorizes Patuxent's budget), and the Baltimore press exert much more power over Patuxent than the Institution does over them. The concept of organization-environment exchanges as the process by which legitimacy (and survival) is negotiated is almost insignificant in the case of Patuxent because the Institution has so little control over the exchanges. Control lies in the Secretary's office and in other components of the task environment. Patuxent's resources, other than its budget, are political. Without key supporters in the Secretary's office, the Governor's office, the legislature, and the judiciary, Patuxent has no claim to legitimacy.

The review of literature for this research found few examples of systematic testing of complex organizational theories. Those that exist are almost exclusively concerned with private organizations, or are in the field of organization ecology. John J. DiIulio, Jr., argues for the development of a science of correctional management, and laments the lack of systematic inquiry into what makes a good correctional manager, or a safe correctional institution. Sociological theory, he argues, has been too taken up with private sector organizations (DiIulio 1991, 11–56).

Research that would further our understanding of what it is that differentiates public from private from other organization types includes the following:

- Systemic descriptions of various organizational types, with particular attention given to components and activities of organizations that conventional wisdom suggest they be classified as public or private. For example, how many different types of prisons are there? Do they differ along dimensions currently used to differentiate public from private organizations? For what types do such distinctions break down? How do prisons differ from other criminal justice agencies, and other public service agencies along those dimensions? Do these descriptions and comparisons suggest other dimensions, or re-conceptualization of ones currently being employed?

- Comparison of organizational development for different types of organizations. How do the creation, maturation, and survival processes of other public organizations (or other "high risk" correctional organizations) compare with those observed at Patuxent. Drug treatment programs in correctional settings or innovative sentencing alternative programs might be candidates for such research. Do these processes and stages differ for private sector organizations, or where do the similarities and differences lie?

Research that would further test theories about how "high risk" organizations survive in hostile environments might include development of typologies for survival threatening situations and comparison of adaptive processes in different types of situations. Again, the current wave of drug treatment programs in corrections comes to mind. For those programs that can be reasonably classified as similar (e.g., Narcotics Anonymous), how frequently do they encounter different types of threatening situations (conflicts over legitimacy vs. conflicts over resources), and are similar adaptive processes at work across programs or across situations? Similar approaches could be taken for other innovative or high risk criminal justice programs.

Case studies such as this one are still a high priority for research on public organizations, because the field is so nascent. Theoretical concepts and distinctions need refining before more systematic testing of hypotheses can take place. While it is difficult to obtain, more "insider" information is needed about political processes that come into play in public policy implementation so that we can be more confident about findings such as those presented in this paper.

Additionally, the practical value of such research needs to be clearly defined and legitimized. Will such research enable those who desire to innovate in public policy arenas to better map out organizational development and survival strategies, or will it help skeptics scrutinize such endeavors better? If policy makers and criminal justice practitioners answer in the affirmative to these questions, then improvements in public policy development and analysis will be realized in both theoretical and real world settings.

The need for case study research notwithstanding, David Garland in *Punishment and Modern Society* (1990) makes a compelling argument for sociological, macro-level inquiry into the forms and nature of punishment, and the intricate links between the institution of punishment and other social institutions.

Multiple Perspectives and Organizational Theory Development

This research began with the functionalist, political economy, and resource dependency theoretical perspectives on organizational adaptation as the bases for studying **how** Patuxent Institution survives. It ended up requiring the neo-institutional perspective to understand **why** Patuxent survives. There is an important lesson here for organizational researchers, especially those interested in organizational development and survival.

There are at least two levels at which organizational adaptive processes take place. At the organization/environment level, interactive and exchange-oriented processes occur—between the organization and its environment (including individuals and other organizations), and between different organization levels. Observing these people, groups, and processes, one can gain insight into how things happen at the organizational level, and how organizations survive. At the societal/institutional level, more subtle processes and exchanges take place, and often over longer periods of time. Ideas change, and ideals change, whereas it is actors and short-lived political phenomena that change at the organizational level. Social, legal, and cultural processes take place at the institutional level, and they affect organizations directly and indirectly. They affect organizations directly through changes in laws, and through bureaucratic, administrative, and professional conventions. They affect organizations indirectly through such phenomena as public tolerance for deviance; popular notions about insanity; and because the people that direct, manage, and work in organizations react to the same, and other, societal pressures and constraints in other avenues of life outside of the organization (in school, in church, in their community) and bring these pressures and conflicts with them to the organization.

Research on organizational development and adaptation that restricts its perspective to the organization/environment level will falter. In order to reach conclusions that make sense, and to fit observations with what we know about individuals, organizations, and society, organizational research must also consider the institutional perspective. The institutional perspective, or the neo-institutional perspective, cannot explain organizational survival in and of itself, however. Organizational survival is as much a day-to-day, short-term process as it is a long-term social and cultural process.

Notes

1. As of 1997, seven states had passed special legislation regarding dangerous sex offenders that allow for their involuntary civil commitment after serving their criminal sentences and over 240

offenders had been involuntarily committed in six of those states (Matson and Lieb 1997, Gabriele 1998).

2. This position no longer exists at Patuxent Institution. It was created by former Director Norma Gluckstern in the early 1980s.

3. The Secretary's office provided this service for all of its criminal justice agencies, but Dr. Gluckstern felt a need to have her own organization do this work. She often found out about proposed legislation before the Secretary's office informed her of it.

4. Several different interview respondents voiced this argument. One respondent, for example, stated specifically that the Jewish legislators from Baltimore needed a place to which violent Jewish criminals could be sent rather than spend their time in other Maryland prisons. Less bias-oriented arguments held that Patuxent existed because legislators and the judiciary in general wanted a place where violent offenders who they felt did not belong in regular prisons (and, who, in the early years were predominantly white and sometimes members of influential families) could be sentenced. The specific motivations behind these arguments are not clear, and this research did not attempt to examine data that might shed light on such arguments.

5. Recall that anti-Patuxent arguments were offered on the basis of cost effectiveness principles, and that Patuxent reacted by conducting its own cost effectiveness studies. The principal actors in these debates could never reach consensus on measures, cost centers, or the bases for comparisons. While the arguments are made over and over, they do not hold as much weight as arguments over much less tangible concepts such as the value of rehabilitation, or Patuxent's contribution to public safety.

6. This operation, which is part of Maryland's State Use Industries program, produces the "stick-on" tags that show proof of vehicle registration, issued by the Maryland Department of Motor Vehicles. It is a somewhat "hi-tech" silk screening operation that trains inmates, pays a higher wage than other inmate workers earn, and competes in a limited market (Maryland State Agencies only may contract with the State Use Industries programs).

Chapter Ten

Epilogue: Patuxent Institution in the 21st Century: From Rehabilitation to Remediation

"If you were to look at any successful psychiatric facility, it's not doing what it was 10 years ago."

Senior Clinician, Patuxent Institution

The research for this book took place toward the end of the 1980s and carried over into the beginning of the 1990s, encompassing an analysis of the history and legitimacy crises of Patuxent Institution since its inception in the 1950s. Ten years have elapsed since the original research, and much has happened at Patuxent. Indeed, a decade is a long time in the life of any major public organization. A decade will witness one or more changes in leadership and management in an organization, as well as changes in key elements of an organization's task environment (elements external to the organization that have direct effects on its mission, operations, and effectiveness). Equally important, a decade will witness significant changes in the less direct but often equally important elements of a public organization's general environment (politics, laws, culture, values, economics, to mention a few).

Patuxent, for certain, is not immune to these influences. In fact, it may be more susceptible to influences from them due to its unique and visible place in the institution of punishment and corrections in America. The year 2001 found Patuxent Institution with an average daily population of 832 (down from its previous level at over 1,100), still providing clinical diagnostic and treatment services to convicted offenders in Maryland, but to a different correctional clientele and in a variety of different ways. Patuxent's enabling legislation (now Title 4 of the Correctional Services Article) mentions "remediation" as the purpose of the institution, not "rehabilitation." In short, Patuxent today is part the Patuxent of yesterday and part new organization based on several well-understood developments and influences, still a unique organization in the history of American penology and still focusing more on treatment than most correctional facilities.

In revisiting the research themes for this book, I updated my understanding of Patuxent Institution according to the key avenues of inquiry developed for the original research – organization mission, administration and operations; environment influences, legitimacy issues and crises; and organizational behavior and response to external influences. I revisited the prison for one week during August 2001[1] to re-acquaint myself with the organization through a series of observations and in-depth interviews. The interviews touched on the following topics: key purpose and mission of Patuxent Institution, changes over time in the mission, reasons for any changes in the mission, current influences in the external environment, and key individuals or events shaping Patuxent over the past 10 years. In all, I conducted 10 formal interviews with staff at different levels of responsibility in several different departments (Director's office, Superintendent's [custody] office, clinicians, work release), and including several external (Board of Patuxent) members. I conducted several less formal interviews with former colleagues from Patuxent,[2] and I observed one inmate therapy group (a therapy group for inmates in diagnostic status at Patuxent). Finally, I obtained several documents from officials at Patuxent and copies of annual reports for almost every year since 1990, and the information gleaned from these also contributed to this epilogue.

Patuxent's Mission in 2001

As is frequently the case in complex organizations, the view of an organization's mission will depend to some extent on the perspective of the organizational actor and on the level of responsibility that actor holds within the organization. So it is and continues to be with Patuxent. We find slight variations in individual's views on the mission of Patuxent depending upon which department one works in (custody and security, education, administration, clinical services, research, and so forth), one's history with Patuxent (employees with more or less experience at Patuxent), and upon one's standing in the organization's hierarchy (line staff or lower level versus supervisors and higher levels). Still, taking such variation into account, when asked most staff at Patuxent exhibit general agreement that treatment of convicted offenders is the main mission of the organization. Several respondents noted the change in Patuxent's enabling legislation to reflect remediation, and not rehabilitation, indicating their sentiment that such a change in the written language is significant (though not explaining precisely what the significance means).[3]

While the notion of treatment is still paramount in most people's minds at Patuxent (and the significance of this alone, after more than 50 years, and after the political turmoil in the late 1980s and early 1990s, should not be overlooked nor understated), the treatment "technology" (or the different procedures and means through which treatment is provided to inmates) is different. According to clinicians at Patuxent, treatment takes a more cognitive than psycho-dynamic approach compared to the past. In other words, compared to a decade ago, treatment at Patuxent is geared more toward the development of life skills that are "portable" (e.g., more likely to stay with and be used by inmates following release from Patuxent). Note here that cognitive approaches were utilized at Patuxent in years past, but earlier approaches to treatment and therapy were more eclectic, depending on the skills of the therapist and the "culture" of the treatment unit. Now, in keeping not only with a desire to develop skills and attitudes that stay with inmates beyond therapy that takes place behind the prison walls, but also with the desire to transfer Patuxent's treatment programs to other parts of the Maryland correctional system (the Division of Correction, Parole and Probation, Department of Mental Health), Patuxent places more focus on cognitive approaches to behavioral change.

Patuxent also provides treatment to several distinctly different populations, which represents a significant departure from prior practices. In the past, the key focus of Patuxent's treatment program (diagnostics, treatment, release preparation) was on "Eligible Persons" (EPs, a category of convicted offender defined in the Institution's enabling legislation), and the focus was on adult male EPs. Now Patuxent offers treatment to male, female, and youth EPs, as well as to inmates in a separate mental health unit (with a supplementary mental health "step down" unit), inmates in separate male and female drug treatment programs, inmates in a separate program called ROTC (Regimented Offender Treatment Center), and inmates in a separate work skills training program coordinated with the Division of Corrections. Thus, whereas there was one main approach to inmate treatment in the past (focused on EP's but actually embodying several different treatment programs such as sex offender treatment, separate female EP program), Patuxent Institution now manages several programmatically different treatment regimens for several different populations (or categories of inmates), and in conjunction with several different component agencies within the Maryland Department of Public Safety and Correctional Services. Table 6 below shows a comparison the Patuxent Institution inmate population in fiscal years 1991 and 2000, to illustrate these differences.

Several other mission-related comments are worth noting here. Under the current administration, Patuxent clinicians have less influence over the Institution's decisions regarding inmates' progress in treatment, attainment of "statuses" (privileges) of various kinds, and eventual release to community-based programming. In prior years, clinicians made recommendations to the Board of Review and took part in meetings at which decisions regarding inmates were

Table 6
Summary of Patuxent Treatment Programs—1991 and 2000

	1991	2000
Adult Eligible Persons	n = 518	n = 244
Male	93%	78%
Female	7%	22%
African American	64%	65%
Caucasian	36%[a]	35%
Average (mean) age	32.8	27.4
Most Serious Offense[b]		
Murder, Homicide, Manslaughter	39%	41%
Rape, Sex Offenses	16%	9%
Kidnapping, Robbery, Assault	28%	17%
Arson, Burglary, Weapons Offenses	7%	7%[c]
Other Offenses	10%	26%[d]
Average Sentence (in years)[e]	27.7	23.5
Youth Eligible Persons		n = 142
Male		96%
Female		4%
African American		82%
Caucasian		18%
Average (mean) age		19.9[f]
Most Serious Offense[b]		
Murder, Homicide, Manslaughter		30%
Rape, Sex Offenses		3%
Kidnapping, Robbery, Assault		24%
Arson, Burglary, Weapons Offenses		1%
Other Offenses		42%
Other Treatment Programs		
Women's Intensive Treatment[g]		
Horticultural Therapy Program		18 certificates awarded
Mental Health Transition Unit		271 admissions, 23 per month 281 discharged Average stay = 240 days
Regimented Offender Treatment Center (ROTC)		624 men admitted 154 women admitted

[a] The 1991 Annual Report noted two individuals with race "unknown." [b] Offense for which the individual was committed to incarceration. [c] Includes burglary, arson, and larceny; weapons offenses not identified. [d] Includes 7% drug offenses. [e] Excludes individuals with life sentences; 2000 report figure estimated from grouped data. [f] Estimated from grouped data. [g] No program data reported.

made. Several procedural adjustments have been made which still have clinicians making recommendations to the Board but with less influence on or active participation in the deliberations of the Board.

Finally, my original research made reference to possible hidden or informal (and political) aspects to Patuxent's mission (e.g., providing a correctional option that allowed judges to sentence white offenders to a place where they could be protected from the harshness and violence of the Division of Correction). While my recent visit to Patuxent did not address this issue directly, some Institution staff repeated this belief (though not suggesting the prison was built expressly for that purpose), despite recent experience that suggests otherwise.[4]

Patuxent Procedures in 2001

Procedural changes have taken place at Patuxent Institution over the past decade, influenced mostly by legislative changes and their immediate impact on Institution operations. Now special treatment populations (e.g., youth, women) are enumerated in the law, there is a cap on the number of Eligible Persons that can be at Patuxent (350), there is more community input into admissions and release decisions, there are stricter release criteria (and less direct influence of clinicians on release decisions). Now the Governor's signature is required to grant parole or release to inmates serving life sentences. Generally, a conservative approach to release practices and decisions prevails.

As a result of these procedural changes, Patuxent's inmate population has changed. Different types of inmates are admitted into Patuxent Institution, they stay longer than they used to, and the diverse population presents a special set of problems that did not previously exist at Patuxent. Recall, for example, the prevailing current view that the youth EPs present behavioral problems (aggression, resistance to the prison regimen) than the adult male population.

Patuxent's External Environment in 2001

The organizations and individuals in Patuxent Institution's external environment that exert the most influence on its mission and operations have changed little over the decades. The influence of the Executive Branch (Governor's Office) is paramount, as is that of the legislature. As noted, the Governor must sign for release of any inmates serving life sentences, the Governor appoints the Secretary of Public Safety and Correctional Services (who oversees Patuxent, and who appoints the Director of Patuxent Institution); and the legislature creates the legislative authority and boundaries under which the Institution operates. In the present day, due to the diversity of programming at Patuxent, top officials in the Division of Correction and the Division of Mental Health have more, albeit indirect, influence over Patuxent than they used to, because Patuxent's mission is viewed in part as developing programs and training that will be of use to those organizations, and because Patuxent provides treatment to populations in those organizations.

While these key organizations and individuals exhibit influence over Patuxent Institution, the less official influences (e.g., the public, the press, advocacy groups) in sum exert less influence than they did in years past. There is a greater influence of citizen members on Patuxent's Board, but the role of the press and other victim's advocate groups is not as prominent as it used to be.

Key Events Affecting Patuxent Institution

The original research for this book focused on several key events in this history of Patuxent Institution that had direct and significant influences on the historical development of this particular prison as a public organization. The subsequent research that provides the basis for this Epilogue found only one incident in the past 10 years that may qualify as a significant public event with the potential for changing Patuxent in significant ways. In 1998, a Patuxent inmate who had absconded from work release was killed in a shoot-out with police in Montana. This incident produced a brief flurry of news reports and discussions about Patuxent, but it died down quickly with no repercussions for Patuxent.

Final Words

Today, as Patuxent Institution nears its fiftieth birthday, it is characterized as much by stability as it is by change and adaptation. Patuxent Institution continues to provide clinically oriented treatment to serious and violent convicted felons in Maryland, with several hundred under treatment on any given day. Today, however, Patuxent Institution provides treatment to a different type and a broader range of offenders compared to the "defective delinquents" it was created to serve in the first place. While the number of individuals in treatment at Patuxent amounts to a small percentage of the incarcerated population in Maryland (and even though the benefit for the larger correctional system in the State is not truly known), Patuxent remains this country's largest and longest-running innovation in corrections. So long as the Institution remains safe, quiet, and free from serious controversy, Patuxent is likely to continue in this vein.

The longevity of Patuxent Institution notwithstanding, it has endured numerous threats, crises, and interruptions to its treatment mission and regimen, the accumulation of which has brought significant change. Today, Patuxent exists as an incubator for treatment and training programs for special correctional populations. In the eyes of some, this represents a long, slow trail to eventual demise, as the core clinical treatment program is further and further diluted. To others, this represents necessary change in the face of admitted failures and political realities.

As the future unfolds for Patuxent, and for the corrections and punishment conglomerate in America, we should hope that research continues along these lines—research aimed at understanding correctional institutions, and correctional policy, in the context of institutional and environmental influences, historically, philosophically, and operationally. The themes found in this historical case study of Patuxent Institution certainly have made some contribution and should continue to hold the interest of researchers and practitioners alike. These include (and are certainly not limited to): the dynamic between external influence on prisons and managerial control from within, the tension between treatment and punishment philosophies, and the "uneasy compromise" between the jailers and the jailed.

February 2004

Notes

1. This research was conducted with the review and approval of the University of Illinois at Chicago Institutional Review Board (IRB). The author extends his sincere thanks to former Patuxent Institution Director Richard Rosenblatt, current Director Dr. Randall Nero, Dr. Richard Craig, and many other Patuxent staff who agreed to meet and talk with me during my visit.

2. In other words, several of the interviews I conducted were not pre-arranged; they took place as schedules permitted and depending on who I encountered during the week of my visit. Each unplanned interview was conducted under the conditions of informed consent according to the approved research protocol.

3. I suspect the new language reflects a political shift away from the less accepted term, "rehabilitation," to a more palatable term, "remediation," which suggests treatment and change but avoids popular notions of rehabilitation as "coddling" or pursuit of the unattainable. It also reflects, as Dr. Nero points out, a focus on addressing behavioral deficits associated with prior criminal behavior (communication from Dr. Nero, July 7, 2003).

4. According to data provided by the Institution (communication with Dr. Nero, July 8, 2003), African Americans and Caucasians comprise similar percentages in the Patuxent and Maryland DOC populations (approximately 77 percent and 23 percent, respectively), and the same holds true for women (approximately 70 percent African American women and 30 percent Caucasian women in both populations). The annual reports and statistical summaries obtained for this research for early years of Patuxent Institution do not distinguish race/ethnicity of offenders diagnosed, admitted, treated, and released, so it was not possible to determine whether these percentages had changed over time.

Appendix A

Historical Timeline for Patuxent Institution

1843 M'Naghten Rule establishing legal standard for insanity established in English Common Law.

1888 *Spencer v. State,* applied M'Naghten Rule in Maryland, providing the legal basis for the insanity defense.

1929 Defective Delinquent statute introduced in Maryland, vetoed by Governor Ritchie.

1931 John W. Anderson murdered by Herman Webb Duker in Baltimore, Judge Joseph N. Ullman sentences Duker to death, sentence commuted to life by Governor Ritchie within one year.

1948 Duker's parole hearing, Commission to Study Medico-Legal Psychiatry presents its report to the Maryland Legislature.

1949 Division of Correction Advisory Board delivers its report on mentally defective inmates, public hearings held to reconcile Commission and Advisory Board reports, memorandum of agreement drafted, Committee on Medico-Legal Procedure established.

1950 Maryland Legislative Council publishes Report #29, "An Indeterminate Sentence Law for Defective Delinquents."

1951 Maryland Legislature enacts Article 31-B, creating and funding Patuxent Institution.

1955 Patuxent Institution opens its doors amidst controversy, admits first inmates, followed by a succession of legal challenges.

1960 Thomsen Commission investigates Patuxent, Patuxent moved out from under the DOC, now reports to Governor through a governing board, Article 31-B amended regarding defective delinquency re-hearings for inmates.

1964 Second Thomsen Commission, under Governor Tawes, investigates Patuxent, found a significant number of inmates with short sentences.

1966 Musgrove case decided in Montgomery County, MD, fuels problems relating to "refusers" (inmates transferred to Patuxent who refused participation on diagnostic procedures).

1967 Michaelson Commission investigates Patuxent.

1970 Mandel is Governor, Gordon Lalley appointed first Secretary of Public Safety and Transportation.

1970–71 Turmoil and tension at Patuxent, legal challenges continue, Patuxent administration troubled, Article 31-B challenged in federal court (*McNeil v. Director*), eventually upheld, riot at Patuxent in February 1971.

1972 Miller-Watts decision leads to changes in disciplinary procedures at Patuxent, later reversed in appeals court, 44 "refusers" released due to district court case in Montgomery County, MD.

1973 U.S. Supreme Court upholds indeterminate sentence.

1974 Successful appeal of "refusers" case (1972) results in return of 44 "refusers" to Patuxent, "mass escape" (6 inmates) in June, young inmate killed in separate incident, inmates take over school building in November, state police arrive with tanks and quell the disturbance.

1975 Patuxent's founding Director, Harold Boslow, retires, J.B. Hardy appointed Director.

1976 Maryland legislature commissions study of Patuxent by Contract Research Corporation, Commission to Evaluate and Coordinate Aggressive Offender Treatment at Patuxent formed, chaired by Alan Wilner.

1977 Article 31-B revised, now is "Eligible Person" statute.

1978 Gordon Kamka appointed Secretary of Public Safety and Correctional Services.

1979 Norma Gluckstern appointed Director of Patuxent Institution.

1981 Kamka resigns as Secretary, Schmidt appointed.

1982 Double-celling begins at Patuxent.

1983 Stephanie Roper Committee lobbies for restrictions on parole for lifers with success, Governor must sign parole for lifers.

1984 Frank Hall appointed Secretary of Public Safety and Correctional Services.

1988 Presidential election, Willie Horton becomes a campaign issue; investigation made into Patuxent's parole and community release practices, Norma Gluckstern leaves, Dr. Joseph Henneberry appointed Director of Patuxent.

1989 Parole practices change at Patuxent, Maryland legislature commissions evaluation of Patuxent by Abt Associates.

1991 Abt Associates releases report on Patuxent, finds no differences in recidivism rates between Patuxent and DOC parolees, Article 31-B amended, Patuxent continues operations, female inmates admitted to Patuxent.

1994 Article 31-B amended to incorporate "remediation" programs for youth, Patuxent Institute Youth Program created, inter-agency agreement developed between Patuxent and the Correctional Mental Health Center at Patuxent and the Maryland Department of Mental Health and Hygiene, Regimented Offender Treatment Center (ROTC) established at Patuxent.

1995 Patuxent receives funding from the National Institute of Drug Abuse (NIDA) for a new program, "Effective Addiction Treatments for Female Offenders, a cooperative effort with the Maryland Correctional Institution for Women, Horticultural Therapy Program" funded by the Bureau of Justice Assistance, Psychological Testing Center established at Patuxent.

1997 Secretary of Public Safety and Correctional Services Secretary Bishop Robinson creates new position—Director of

Mental Health Services. Patuxent Director Joseph Henneberry appointed to the position in addition to his role as Director of Patuxent.

1999 Patuxent's enabling law (originally Article 31-B) re-located under Title 4 of the new Correctional Services Article, program initiated to educate the Maryland judiciary about Patuxent, Patuxent youth program expands.

2000 Richard Rosenblatt appointed Director of Patuxent Institution following the resignation of Dr. Henneberry, Mental Health Transition Unit established at Patuxent, including a "step-down" unit.

Appendix B

A Note on Research Methods

Historical case study research presents special methodological and epistemological challenges for the social science researcher. Collecting evidence (methodology) that goes decades back in time is difficult enough, but making sense of the data collected and presenting the result as "knowledge" (epistemology) is even more difficult. Drawing from the key methodological work of Robert Yin and Barry Turner this appendix articulates how data were collected and how a large volume of largely qualitative data were turned into theory from the ground up in this research.

Robert Yin, in *Case Study Research,* defines a case study as "an empirical inquiry that investigates a contemporary phenomenon within its real-life context; when the boundaries between phenomenon and context are not clearly evident; and in which multiple sources of evidence are used" (Yin 1984, 23). Yin also lists five important components of case study research design:

1. Study questions,
2. Propositions,
3. Unit(s) of analysis,
4. Logic linking data to the propositions, and
5. Criteria for interpreting findings. (Yin 1984, 29)

This research utilized the case study method. Patuxent Institution is not so much a contemporary phenomenon (since it has been in existence for over 40 years) as it is a unique and revelatory one. No prison in the country or the world has the combined qualities of Patuxent Institution (legislative mandate to rehabilitate, administrative control over admissions and releases, capacity over 600, maximum-security classification), and few have ever had to justify their existence on treatment grounds. The literature on organizations, especially on public and criminal justice organizations, contains few empirical studies of adaptability and survival. Kaufman's (1976) study of federal agencies, Kimberly's (1975) study of rehabilitation workshops, and Bowman and Snyder's (1985) study of the Selective Service System represent the empirical works most relevant to this study.

Theoretical discussions about organizational adaptation and survival are more numerous (for example, Thompson 1967, Bidwell and Kasarda 1985, Kimberly and Miles 1980, Pfeffer 1982, Pfeffer and Salancik 1978, Selznick 1949), but many of the propositions in these works remain untested; they have not been subjected to systematic examination.

This case study research project provides two valuable additions to the study of public organizations:

1. It examines some of the general hypotheses regarding organizational adaptation and organization-environment interaction, and

2. It provides additional data regarding the survival of one organization, which adds to the general body of knowledge about public organizations.

As Yin points out, the potential for a case study to make a significant contribution to a body of knowledge rests on its research design, on "...the logical sequence that links empirical data to the research questions, and to conclusions..." (Yin 1984, 28). This appendix outlines that logical sequence for this research. It discusses the concepts and variables investigated and presents the underlying model and assumptions. The data collection and analysis methods are reviewed. In this manner, the sequence of concept definition, to model development and hypothesis formulation, and to research techniques is explained. The appendix concludes with a discussion of the limitations to this research.

Concepts and Variables for the Case Study

This research relied strongly on three sets of concepts. All were interrelated but each referred to different perspectives on organizational activity. One set of concepts relates to the organization itself, another to the (task) environment surrounding the organization, and the third to interaction between the organization and its environment. Since these concepts dominate the sociological literature on organizations and can often be confusing (typically, they are discussed in different ways by different researchers), the following pages lay out in detail how these concepts were developed and how they related to the case study of Patuxent.

The Organization as a Sociological Phenomenon

Six concepts relating to organizations as distinct entities are considered here, beginning with the concept of public organization. Patuxent has characteristics that most students of organizations would recognize as "public." Wamsly and Zald (1973) present political and economic bases for the definition of public organizations. In the political sense, public organizations are part of the State, and are perceived as belonging to or owned by the State and its citizens. Participation by the State and citizenry in how public organizations' goals are set, how resources are allocated, and how they obtain legitimacy sets public organizations apart from private organizations. Similarly, in the economic sense, public organizations depend on the public (usually through elected representatives) for financing. The relationship between cost (or price) and the utility of public organizations is often overshadowed by questions of legitimacy. Private organizations are more closely linked to marketplaces and strict economic factors (Wamsly and Zald 1973, 7).

Rainey, Backoff, and Levine (1983) follow the Wamsly and Zald approach to defining public organizations on economic and political bases, but use a broader framework. Public organizations differ from private organizations by environmental factors (less exposure to economic markets, more legal and formal constraints, and greater influence of politics); organization-environment transactions (coercive nature of public organizations, greater potential for public organizations to have an impact on the public, greater scrutiny and expectations by the public, public or quasi-public nature of goals or services provided); and internal structure and processes (diversity and conflict of goals, vagueness of evaluation criteria, weaker role of administrators due to formal rules and greater visibility, tending toward dysfunctioning such as red tape, buck passing, or lack of innovativeness) (Rainey, Backoff, and Levine 1983, 96–97).

Patuxent Institution, like all state prisons, is supported by taxes (save for the occasional donation of books, materials, or equipment for inmates and educational purposes, all of which must be approved by state officials) and is a legislatively mandated agency in the State of Maryland Department of Public Safety and Correctional Services. Like other prisons, it is reviewed periodically (annually) by legislative committees, is open to public scrutiny (by the press, grand juries, other state officials and interest groups), and its records and files are part of the public record (not including individual personnel and inmate data protected by privacy laws). Patuxent's goals (confinement, punishment, and treatment) conflict and evaluation criteria are vague. Regular statistics on cost effectiveness and recidivism are produced (the data most requested by the public and legislature), though such data on Patuxent lack comparability to other prisons due to a variety of factors relating to its inmate population and its operations. Patuxent Institution produces no tangible product, only treated inmates and "public safety." By most standards, and certainly by the criteria suggested by Wamsly and Zald, and Rainey, Patuxent Institution is a public organization.

The five other concepts relating to organizations as distinct entities that concern this research are organization function, culture, structure, power, and life cycle (or development). Each is a phenomenon that can figure significantly in an organization's survival.

Organization function concerns the general and specific roles an organization plays in society. Parsons (and many others) would argue that the general functions of an organization are to mobilize individuals toward the attainment of specific goals and products that are used by other organizations and social systems. He would argue further that a primary goal of organizations is to link individuals to the larger social structures through the goal-oriented activity (Parsons 1965, 19). Katz and Kahn adopt much of the Parsonian open-system perspective on the function of organizations, though from the social psychological exchange perspective which defines organizations as structures for repeated patterned activities that turn input into output, focusing more on the activities than on the goal(s) under which they are subsumed (Katz and Kahn 1966, 17). They adopt a four-way characterization of organization functions very similar to Parsons': productive/economic, maintenance, adaptive/political, and managerial (Katz and Kahn 1966, 113).

Patuxent Institution functions primarily as an integrative organization, an organization of social control in the narrow sense (Parsons 1965, 46). Its specific function is that most often ascribed to prisons: confinement and public protection. In the case of Patuxent Institution, with its legislative mandate to rehabilitate, the punitive function is mixed with a pattern maintenance function: rehabilitation or resocialization of convicted criminals for their reintegration into society.

Others have attributed latent (or alternative) functions to Patuxent, such as a means for confining dangerous criminals for life in a humane environment (Carney 1985, 3), a humane place for the relatives of powerful and influential people, or a "safety valve" for the housing of troublesome inmates away from the Division of Correction.[1] These will be considered further on. For now, Patuxent Institution's function is defined as that of prisons in general, but it is one prison that gives serious attention to the rehabilitative goal.

The structure of an organization refers to the "...internal differentiation and patterning of relationships..." to organization design and departmentalization (and connectedness) in complex organizations (Thompson 1967, 51). Thompson also includes patterns of coordination and interdependence, and organization hierarchy as components of organization structure (Thompson 1967, 51–65). This research uses this conceptualization of organization structure as a starting point.

For the study of Patuxent Institution, two aspects of organization structure are particularly relevant: boundary spanning, and formal versus informal organization. According to Thompson, boundary spanning units of organizations are "parts of organizations (that) must be interdependent with organizations not subordinated to the organization...and whose function is...not coordination (of variables under control), but *adjustment* to constraints and contingencies not controlled by the organization" (Thompson 1967, 66–67). Schwab, Ungson, and Brown challenge the contingency theory approach to boundary spanning activities (that environment is their primary determinant), but accept the premise that the job of boundary spanners is to "correctly scan and monitor the activities of the task environment" (Schwab, Ungson, and Brown 1985, 76–77). This premise is central to this research. As an organization facing a hostile (and at times unpredictable) task environment, the structure of Patuxent should contain boundary spanning functions that help in the adaptive process.

The works of Selznick (1949), Merton (1957), and March and Simon (1958) suggest that organization structures have formal (planned) and informal (unintended, emergent) aspects, and this is certainly the case for Patuxent. Part of its structure is formal because it is mandated by law (the upper-level management structure, the governing board, client procurement), or because it has a long history with little change. Other aspects of Patuxent's structure have clearly informal characteristics, such as custody-treatment interaction and problem solving, and other information gathering activities. Particular attention is paid in this research to the roles the formal and informal aspects of Patuxent's structure play in the adaptive process.

Organizational culture is an elusive concept, though one that must be addressed in this research since much of what is being examined falls under current discussions in this area. Most definitions of organizational culture are similar to definitions of broader cultures in the sociological or anthropological sense, referring to such elements as beliefs, perspectives, mores, shared meanings, symbols, history, patterns of communication, and so on. In *A Sociology of Organisations*, Eldridge and Crombie define organizational culture as follows:

> The culture of an organisation refers to the unique configuration of norms, values, beliefs, ways of behaving and so on that characterise the manner in which groups and individuals combine to get things done. The distinctiveness of a particular organisation is intimately bound up with the history and the character-building effects of past decisions and past leaders. It is manifested in the folkways, mores, and the ideology to which members defer, as well as the strategic choices made by the organization as a whole. (Eldridge and Crombie 1975, 89)

Beck and Moore, writing about how host cultures link to organizational variables, recognize the limited utility of such broad definitions to the researcher. In their view, it is impossible to completely describe or understand all aspects of a given culture. It is better to identify cultural attributes with particular relevance to the issue at hand, recognizing the vast array of sources of cultural attributes (Beck and Moore, in Frost et al. 1985, 340).

John Van Mannen and Stephen Barley discuss the theory of organizational culture and state the following:

> Culture implies that human behavior is partially prescribed by a collectively created and sustained way of life that cannot be personality based because it is shared by diverse individuals. Neither can a way of life be derived solely from structure, since members of separate collectivities themselves occupy equivalent positions in a structured matrix. Rather, culture points to an

> analysis mediating between deterministic and volunteeristic modes of behavior in organizations. (Van Mannen and Barley, in Frost et al., 1985, 31–32)

They note the distinction between the structural-functional perspective on culture (defining culture as a set of solutions devised by people to meet common problems) and the symbolic and cognitive approaches (culture as collections of negotiated, emergent symbols and meanings), and make the point that the structural-functional definition is more applicable to organizations, which tend to be problem solving social systems (Van Mannen and Barley, in Frost et al. 1985, 33).

Both perspectives are valuable to this research because two distinct aspects of organizational culture are at issue. The first concerns the interaction between the aspects of Patuxent's organizational culture and the broader culture that address the problem of social control. How does Patuxent's perspective (exemplified in written policies as well as individual actions) differ from broader societal perspectives, and how have these perspectives changed over time? The structural-functional perspective examines Patuxent's answer to the problem in comparison to the answer prescribed by the broader culture. The second aspect of organizational culture at issue concerns aspects of Patuxent's culture that determine its reaction to environmental or cultural constraints. The symbolic perspective looks at the myths and perspectives, unifying symbols, and lore called upon to reinforce the rehabilitation goal at Patuxent in reaction to perceived encroachments in that area.

Organizational life cycle refers to a dynamic process of organizational development analogous to the biological life cycle—birth, development, decline, death—with the exception that organizations can experience rebirth. This concept counts organizational history, age, and experiences as important determinants of current state and chances of survival. Kimberly and Miles discuss this concept in depth in *The Organizational Life Cycle*, and use it in the population ecology sense (development of organization types and forms in the aggregate) and at the individual organization level. The life cycle concept, they argue, is imperfect but instructive. It lends a dynamic aspect to organizational analysis in comparison to most other approaches that take organization existence as a given and assume survival as both a goal and an indicator of success.

The organization life cycle concept is important to this research because it provides a general (developmental) perspective for analyzing Patuxent's adaptive behavior that other theoretical approaches and perspectives do not. The life cycle concept suggests that elements present at Patuxent's creation influence how it responds to threatening situations, and that adaptive behavior is evolutionary, that is, present adaptations are influenced by the past and exert influence on future adaptations. The life cycle concept also suggests that Patuxent's history will exhibit periods of growth, stability, decline, and rebirth, and that certain organizational and contextual factors will influence the development. These are important avenues of inquiry in historical research on organizations.

The Organization Environment

This section draws on discussions found in a variety of works on organization environments to define that concept, and to bring other closely related concepts: domain, task environment, to bear on this research. Since this book addresses how Patuxent Institution adapts to certain threats posed by its "environment," it is important to formalize the concept as a part of the general model.

A clear and generally agreed upon definition of "organization environment" is elusive. In *Organization Environments,* Scott notes that:

> ...although there is now consensus on the importance of environment, there is little agreement about how the environment is to be conceived or which of its features are most salient.
>
> Although the concept is widely understood to refer to conditions external to the organization and present in its surrounding context, it is

> necessary to point out that these connotations are misleading when applied to open systems such as organizations...we need to see that organizations incorporate aspects of that (technical) environment into their own systems...institution environments are notoriously invasive. (Meyer and Scott 1983, 15–16)

Thus, organization environments are difficult to define because they are nebulous, at once external and internal to organizations.

Pfeffer and Salancik, major proponents of environment oriented resource dependency theory, offer little in the way of a definition for organization environment, though they stress the cognitive aspect of the concept. In their words:

> In one sense, the environment includes every event in the world which has any effect on the activities or outcomes of the organization. Organization environments are not given realities; they are created through a process of attention and interpretation. (Pfeffer and Salancik 1978, 12–13)

In light of the difficulty of defining organization environment specifically enough to be useful for research, most discussions of the concept refer to the related concepts of domain and task environment proposed by Thompson to incorporate the organization environment notion. Thompson defines domain as "...the points at which the organization is dependent on inputs from the environment." He does not define environment, but defines "task environment" as "...those parts of the environment which are `relevant or potentially relevant to goal setting and attainment' (from Dill 1958) ...those organizations in the environment which make a difference to the organization in question" (the "organization set," from Evan 1966) (Thompson 1967, 28).

These concepts are important for this research. They suggest a conceptualization of environment, if not a definition, that embodies certain critical observable elements. For this research, then, organization environment refers to persons, organizations, ideas, and events outside of the formal boundaries of Patuxent Institution that influence the organization in any way, and that specifically influence the goal of offender treatment.

Conceptualizing Organization-Environment Interactions

This section considers the problem of defining concepts that incorporate the interaction between an organization and its environment. Since this research entails a case study of one organization, the problem is approached from the resource dependency perspective of Pfeffer and Salancik, not from the population ecology perspective of Hannan and Bidwell and Kasarda (Chapter Two discusses the difference between these two perspectives). This section also considers this problem for public organizations, which face different environments than do private organizations.

The writings of Pfeffer and Salancik, Wamsly and Zald, and Thompson provide concepts helpful in developing a research strategy around organization-environment interactions. The specific concepts reviewed here include Thompson's discussion of boundary spanning, and Pfeffer and Salancik's and Wamsly and Zald's (and Thompson's) discussions of constraints and organization adaptation and survival.

Thompson, Pfeffer and Salancik, and Wamsly and Zald all discuss organizations from a resource dependency perspective, though Pfeffer and Salancik place the heaviest emphasis on environmental constraints on organization behavior. For all of these authors, the constraints felt by organizations are major determinants of organization structure and behavior. For Thompson, organizations seek to manage aspects of their task environment that they cannot control by gaining power in a variety of ways (maintaining alternate sources of input, seeking prestige, and other solutions such as cooptation, contracting, coalescing) (Thompson 1967, 37–38). In their discussion of organization environments, Wamsly and Zald argue that organizations do not simply react to their environments, but that exchanges take place through "feedback loops" to the organization (through clientele, advisory committees, inclusion of interest groups in the administrative structure) (Wamsly and Zald 1973, 40).

Pfeffer and Salancik discuss organizational constraints from a different and instructive standpoint: their "functionality" for the organization. They explain that: "Actions can be said to be constrained whenever one response to a given situation is more probable than any other response to the situation, regardless of the actor responding...constraint is present whenever responses to a situation are not random." They explain further that constraints facilitate choices and adaptive processes by limiting choices and promoting consistency, and that this conceptualization of constraints "...explains why individuals account for relatively little variance in the performance and activities of organizational systems" (Pfeffer and Salancik 1978, 14–15). Pfeffer and Salancik draw heavily from Thompson in their discussion of organization dependence on environment, and provide a useful way of viewing constraints as both organizational determinants and problems.

The most important theme in this discussion of organization-environment interactions is that of exchange. Precisely what is exchanged between organizations and environments is difficult to pinpoint, especially in the case of public organizations. It may be a purely economic exchange (certain services for a budgetary increase, or capital improvements), or a less tangible, political exchange (concessions to an interest group for increased visibility or prestige, concessions to a powerful legislative coalition to minimize potential harm). Organizational adaptation is a manifestation of an organization-environment exchange, an organizational reaction to a constraint felt from the environment.

This research focuses on constraints felt by Patuxent Institution, those that were perceived by institutional management as a threat to the treatment mission. Such threats may come from internal (mismanagement of resources, lack of professional standards, unqualified staff) or external sources (legislative effort to revise Patuxent's enabling legislation or to close the Institution, the development of the prisoners' rights movement). This research focuses on external threats to the treatment goal at Patuxent, but recognizes the inseparable link between internal and external threats. For example, poor (internal) management in reaction to an external threat may threaten the treatment goal more than the external threat alone; or external perceptions of inadequate internal management may result in attempts from external sources to modify organizational practices.

In its focus on external threats to Patuxent, this research carefully studies the boundary spanning and exchange activities of Patuxent in relation to its immediate and broader external environment to learn about the organization's adaptive behavior.

A General Model for Studying Organization-Environment Interaction

This section presents a general model for understanding the key elements in this research, and for analyzing Patuxent's adaptive behavior.

Patuxent Institution's core technology (Thompson 1967, 19) includes two primary functions: control and preservation of public safety (deterrence, confinement, punishment), and rehabilitation of violent criminals (as defined by law and observable organizational history).[2] The treatment technology, again using Thompson's terminology, is intensive (drawing upon a variety of techniques to achieve change in an object, Thompson 1967:17) and has a low degree of technical rationality (logical cause-effect relationships). This fact has certain implications for the structure, functioning, efficiency, and nature of power in the organization.

The external component of the research model considers specific and general threats to Patuxent's treatment goal. The appropriate function of imprisonment has been debated since prisons emerged as formal organizations of the State. It can be safely assumed that when a prison such as Patuxent represents the extreme of one side in the debate (pro-rehabilitation or treatment), challenges to its legitimacy will come from proponents of other sides in the debate (pro-punishment or confinement) and from other sectors in society.

The third component of the research model includes the organization-environment interactions that comprise the adaptation Patuxent has made to external threats, and adjustments made in the environment. These will be found in such observable phenomena as formal and informal mechanisms of organization-environment interactions and uses of power, roles and interactions of key actors and dominant coalitions, and the impact of societal events and trends outside of the control of Patuxent Institution.

Assumptions

The general approach taken for this research, and its reliance on the resource dependency perspective on organizations, entails a number of assumptions that must be made explicit. Identifying the underlying assumptions for a research effort provides the reader with a useful perspective for evaluating the research. It serves to keep the researcher mindful of the boundaries within which the research should be conducted and beyond which the findings should not be applied. A clear statement of assumptions will also indicate certain aspects of the research model that may be tested through observation and data collection. A review of assumptions will promote better understanding of the research project and reduce the likelihood of inappropriate generalizations or interpretations.

Certain assumptions are made in this research about the source and temporal sequence of events constituting threats to Patuxent's treatment goal—that these threats originate from external sources, and that they are followed by observable reactions on the part of Patuxent Institution. These assumptions are made for the purpose of stating the general research problem in simple terms. Actually, the existence (or perception) of a threat on the part of Patuxent Institution will go hand-in-hand with the perception on the part of some external actor with a problem regarding the treatment goal (its existence, importance, or implementation). It may also be that the perception on the outsider's part is the result of the actions of Patuxent Institution (staff or inmates). Organization problems are emergent phenomena, developing from constant interaction between internal and environmental factors. To study them, one must pick a point of perspective to define the research problem and strategy. In this instance, the focus is on the perception of a threat and the organization's reaction to it, while it is understood that different factors and chains of events contribute to the development of the perception.

Assumptions are made in this research about the actual existence of threats to Patuxent's treatment goal. It would be impossible to determine the extent to which a threat's seriousness is real or imagined. Put another way, to what extent is a threat to Patuxent's treatment goal the result of external forces or part of the Institutional culture that reinforces the treatment goal for employees by focusing attention on outside dangers? To a certain extent the actions of external actors can be documented, but since Patuxent has not been forced to change its treatment goal in any significant way, it is hard to tell whether any threat was really potentially fatal. This research assumes that Patuxent faced some serious threats to its treatment goal over the years, and considers the assessment of seriousness in its methodology, but does not attempt to resolve the issue definitively.

General assumptions relating to the conflict and open-systems perspective are also made in this research. Generally, events and social forces occurring outside of Patuxent are assumed to have significant impact on its internal operations and relationships, and vice versa: Patuxent will in some way affect its outside environment. While this research seeks to explain how these exchanges occur in a few specific instances, the "openness" of prison-society interactions is not questioned. It is also assumed that conflict rather than consensus is the best description of the exchange between Patuxent and its environment regarding its treatment goal. The conflicting goals operating within Patuxent (treatment and control), coupled with society's conflict over punishment (retribution versus deterrence versus rehabilitation versus isolation), set the stage for many conflicts between Patuxent and its environment. Conflict and consensus are matters of degree for organizations and environments, coexisting and varying over time, across actors and situations. The general perspective of this research focuses on Patuxent's conflict with its environment, understanding that consensus exists as well.

Perspective of the Research

This research examines Patuxent's survival primarily from the subject's (organization's) perspective. It explores the question of how Patuxent survived threats perceived to be inimical to its existence, how Patuxent adjusted and adapted to the threats, and the impact of these adaptations on the Institution. The perspectives of Patuxent's immediate environment (criminal justice and legal actors in the State of Maryland) and the broader social environment (professionals, national figures, the media, and the public) are considered in the analysis. Patuxent is the focal point for this inquiry into organizational adaptation.

Research Methods

This is a case study of Patuxent Institution's response to threats from its environment. Some important aspects of this case study must be delineated. It is a *historical* case study; it considers Patuxent's response to different threats at different points in time. As such, it considers multiple "cases" of threats and, consequently, various kinds of threats.

Data Collection

This research relied on multiple sources of information and methods of data collection, not only to cover the numerous avenues of inquiry, but also as a means of cross-checking findings from different methods.

Archival research of historical documents (news media, published papers and unpublished manuscripts of Patuxent employees, memos and documents from administrative files, Maryland statutes, legislative records, case law) provided much of the information concerning Patuxent's history and development. This research revealed the legislative intent behind Patuxent's creation, early organizational design and treatment methods, and the development of the Institution.

Interviews with past and present executives and administrative staff, and with significant actors in Patuxent's external environment, provided information concerning the major threats faced by Patuxent. Seventeen interviews were conducted initially (from 1986 to 1990), lasting from one to three hours each.[3] Each interview was taped and transcribed. The researcher followed an interview schedule, which was modified slightly for the type of informant (clinical or custody staff, current or past employee, insider or outsider). Interviewing multiple actors involved in the major threatening events, and reviewing documented accounts served as validating methods for these interviews. The list of interview subjects includes:

- Directors of Patuxent,
- Associate Directors and other administrators,
- advisory board members,
- members of the Maryland legislature,
- judges,
- correctional officers, and
- other significant actors in Patuxent's history and environment.

The interviews focused on the most threatening challenges faced by Patuxent, and were structured to obtain the following information from subjects:

- their views on Patuxent (philosophy and practices, operations, staff, and inmates),
- the significant actors in the event,
- the major issues involved,
- decisions and actions taken, and
- the outcome of the struggle.

Observations of Patuxent in action—of the dealings executives and middle managers have with significant external actors—provided additional information regarding the strategies used by Patuxent to manage troublesome or threatening situations. The author was a member of the Patuxent Institution administrative staff from April 1984 through June 1987, and in that capacity had access to meetings, documents, correspondence, and actors in such situations. He was provided similar access to meetings and documents during the course of this research, though not continuously.

Data Analysis

The foundations of this research have been presented in both the literature review and in the discussion of theoretical concepts in this chapter. A general hypothesis regarding the factors influencing Patuxent's reaction to threatening situations was also offered. This research utilized the "grounded theory" approach to theory development described by Glaser and Strauss (1967) and Turner (1981, 1983). In that approach, concepts (and hypothesized relationships among them) emerge from the collection of qualitative data, and from a continual process of analysis and refinement as field work progresses.

Eventually, a theory of how Patuxent has survived as a treatment-oriented prison "emerged" from the data.

The following explanation reveals how this approach increases internal validity and ensures that findings relevant to the substantive area of inquiry are produced:

First, plausible explanations and concepts related to Patuxent's survival strategies were gleaned from existing literature on complex public organizations (see the literature review above). In this manner, a general understanding of current knowledge relating to organizational survival was obtained, and relevant concepts were identified.

Next, data were collected through the various methods described and detailed sets of field and concept development notes were maintained. The field notes and transcribed interviews were reviewed periodically, and concepts defined from them. As the research progressed, the concepts were refined, plausible explanations formulated, and then further examined through review of new materials and re-reading of the concept notes.

For example, field notes from interviews and observations contain references to how key actors in Patuxent's environment viewed their roles in evaluating, criticizing, or shaping the Institution. For example, one legislator, a key figure in many of the debates surrounding Patuxent, explained how he was concerned with the "bottom line," how much Patuxent costs the taxpayers of Maryland, and how well it protects the public from violent criminals. When asked whether he was concerned about treatment philosophy and practices at Patuxent, he replied that he was not knowledgeable regarding clinical matters and did not want to try and tell the experts how to do their business. Responses to this line of inquiry from other interview subjects were located and compared. In this manner, a picture of how legislators and others focused their attention on the Institution emerged.

Once an explanation of how Patuxent survived threats to its legitimacy and survival was developed, it was compared to theories in the existing literature on organization survival. This comparison is presented in the final chapter, and includes a discussion of how adequately current theories explain organizational survival, and the contributions this research makes in this substantive area.

Limitations

The choices of a particular research topic and method of inquiry always entail certain limitations. A discussion of limits to this research is essential to provide the reader with adequate information upon which to gauge the work presented. This section discusses three limitations of this historical case study of Patuxent Institution: limitations of the case study method, of the specific data collection methods employed, and of the author's perspective.

Limitations of the Case Study Method

The most frequently mentioned criticism of the case study method is that of the inability to generalize from findings (Forcese and Richer 1973, Yin 1984). Depending on the exact nature of the case study, one or a few points of observation will be made and usually will produce qualitative data from a non-random sample. This criticism is concerned with inappropriate use of case study findings, not with the case study method itself. When the case study method is used appropriately, findings are useful as: (1) addition of rich descriptive detail to a body of knowledge, and (2) as a single-case examination of theory regarding a phenomenon—in this case the survival of public organizations. Yin makes the following important points concerning this criticism of the case study method:

> While it is true that case study findings usually cannot be generalized to populations or universes, they are generalizable to theoretical propositions;

> the goal is to expand and generalize in the theoretical realm, not in the statistical realm. (Yin 1984, 21)

Limitations to Data Collection Methods

The limitations of the three data collection methods used for this research — archival research, interviews, and observations — are critical since they entail a potential loss of information. Four factors that produce limitations for each method include lack of time and other resources, difficulty of recollecting details about events (on the parts of interview subjects and the observer/author), other difficulties in reconstructing historical events, and lack of accessibility to information and materials.

The list of potential interview subjects numbered close to 100 (based on the author's contacts and on archival research that suggested subjects for interviews). Time and resources did not permit such an extensive endeavor, nor were all of the potential subjects available. Additionally, the volume of field notes that would be produced from so many interviews would make their analysis unmanageable. For these reasons, a total of 17 subjects were interviewed initially, followed by 10 interviews at the latter stages of the research. While this small sample size undoubtedly resulted in the loss of important information, part of this loss was made up through other interviews and through the archival research and observations.

Many of the interview subjects were asked to recall events or perceptions from 10 to 30 years in the past, a difficult task. Additionally, many respondents were either retired or had been away from Patuxent for many years. Their ability to recollect events and thoughts might be suspect. This limitation was mitigated by the fact that the interviews focused on major events in the history of Patuxent Institution, and it is assumed that recall for those events was greater than it would be for minor or daily occurrences. The author rarely compiled field notes during his three and one-half years as a member of the Patuxent staff (this research was not contemplated when he began working there). He, too, was forced to recall events and his own perceptions.

Reconstruction of historical events is difficult for other reasons. Regardless of the data collection method (or combination of methods) used, they fail to capture the complexity of issues and emotions operating at the time of the event or events under scrutiny. This is a universal measurement problem, but it is accentuated in this case because of the emotional and political nature of Patuxent's struggle to survive. The material presented in this paper portrays simplified versions of some complex issues and highly charged events in the history of Patuxent.

Lack of accessibility also presented problems for this research. Patuxent Institution never had an official historian, though a few employees (who had worked there for over 20 years) had the presence of mind to save many documents (reports, memoranda, letters, rules, regulations, procedures). Some of the outside actors (judges, inmates, legislators) also saved valuable materials. Still, some historical material was lost over the years, and no consistent rule was followed regarding what was recorded and saved at Patuxent.

Some additional comments regarding the interview method are necessary. Uniformity across interview questions and conditions was lacking, for reasons both necessary and due to unpredictable events. Interview subjects varied in their length of association with Patuxent and, thus, in their impressions and knowledge about the events covered by this research. Similarly, some subjects worked in areas that determined their limited responses (in the halfway house or on the custodial force, for example). Interview schedules were geared to the subjects, and a certain combination of questions was asked depending on the subject's length of association, affiliation, and job type with Patuxent. Uniform questions were not asked of subjects, and the amount of information gained from interviews varied greatly. This limits the comparability of data across subjects, but not necessarily the value of the data obtained.

The conditions under which interviews were conducted varied. Some were conducted in the home of the respondent in a relaxed atmosphere with few interruptions. Others were conducted in the respondent's place of business, and were characterized by more interruptions or distractions than those conducted in homes. These conditions produced variations in the amount and quality of information obtained from the interviews, more than the variations in the interview schedules.

Limitations to the Author's Perspective

This particular topic, the perspectives and potential biases of the researcher/author, is critical for case studies that rely on observations. Methodological controls can be developed to reduce the likelihood of bias (e.g., using other observers, using checks on observers, using other data sources), but the bias cannot be eliminated. It is the researcher's duty to inform the reader about his or her own biases.

The primary point to be made in this regard concerns the researcher's three-year employment at Patuxent Institution. He was hired as the Institution's first full-time researcher in April 1984 and worked in that capacity until June 1987. Two aspects of his employment are important: his position in the administrative structure and hierarchy, and his personal opinion regarding the functions and goals of Patuxent Institution.

As the Research Director at Patuxent, the author reported directly to the chief executive, the Director of Patuxent Institution. Administratively, no other bureaucratic levels separated him from top management. He worked with the other top-level managers (Director of Custody, Director of Treatment, administrative head, Director of Education, Director of the Halfway House) on all major institutional projects and problems. In this position, he developed an administrator's perspective on Patuxent Institution, as opposed to the perspectives of line workers (officers, clinicians, secretaries) and lower-level management (unit managers, team leaders, captains and lieutenants). This perspective poses the danger of biasing his views on the effectiveness of administrative policies and actions, or ignoring other perspectives on major events. This bias was countered in two ways. During his employment the researcher sought out others from line and lower-management staff and tried to elicit their perspectives on issues of the day. Similarly, the interviews for this research included subjects who had held line positions at some point during their association with Patuxent.

As is the case with most upper-level employees in complex organizations, the author adopted many of the views of Patuxent's management, by choice or by socialization processes. He accepted as legitimate Patuxent's treatment goal and practices, while maintaining as objective and critical a perspective as was politically and managerially feasible. This acceptance of the treatment goal has clear implications for this research. It brings the dangers of (1) adopting the Patuxent view on threats, (2) ignoring other perspectives on Patuxent, and (3) over-emphasizing the "success" of Patuxent's adaptive strategies. These dangers were also addressed and to some degree countered through multiple data sources and respondents. Additionally, the author left Patuxent as the research project began, and was less constrained by the political dangers of anti-Patuxent views.

In summary, the best strategy for lessening the impact of the limitations and biases that come into play in any research endeavor is to not claim the findings are more than they really are, to not generalize outside the case, and to not ignore or avoid the issue of personal bias. No attempt is made in this research to apply the findings beyond Patuxent Institution, except in the exploratory theoretical sense, and every attempt is made to familiarize the reader with the author's perspective and biases (and with those of others). Patuxent Institution presents a unique opportunity to consider important issues in theory and research on the adaptive behavior of public organizations, primarily because it is an extreme and revelatory case, not because it represents other prisons or public organizations. The research design and methods were designed with this goal in mind; no deviations from them are attempted.

Notes

1. The author heard these opinions expressed by Patuxent staff on various occasions. These staff were not involved in the creation of Patuxent, and were perhaps reflecting on their opinions regarding some of Patuxent's rare and "sensational" cases.

2. These goals are often in conflict at Patuxent, a major factor in the debates over Patuxent's legitimacy.

3. Three of these interviews were conducted as part of the development of the proposal for this research. Ten additional interviews were conducted with Patuxent staff and Citizens Review Board members during the summer of 2000, which formed the basis of the Epilogue for this book.

Appendix C

Patuxent Institution Organization Chart

Patuxent Institution - Organization Chart*

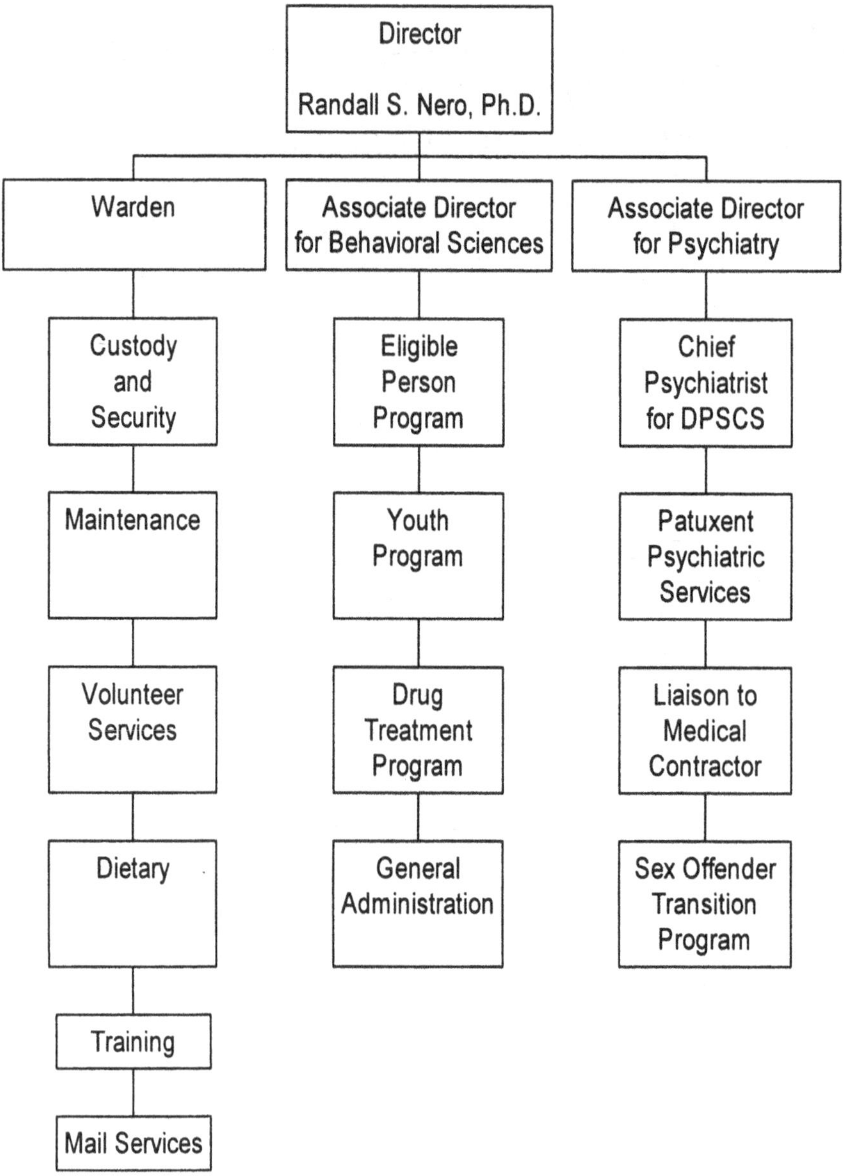

***Source: adapted from Patuxent Institution Annual Report 2002.**

Bibliography

Aldrich, Howard E. *Organizations and Environments*. Englewood Cliffs, NJ: Prentice-Hall, 1979.

American Civil Liberties Union. "ACLU Files Legal Challenge to Solitary Confinement of Sex Offenders Awaiting Civil Commitment Trials in Iowa." New York: *ACLU News*, November 29, 2001.

Barnard, Chester. *The Functions of the Executive*. Cambridge, MA: Harvard University Press, 1938.

Bazelon, David L. *Questioning Authority*. New York: Alfred A. Knopf, 1988.

Bidwell, Charles E., and John D. Kasarda. *The Organization and Its Ecosystem*. Greenwich, CN: JAI Press, Inc., 1985.

Blumstein, A., and J. Cohen. "A Theory of the Stability of Punishment." *Journal of Criminology, Criminal Law and Police Science*, 63(2) (1973): 198–207.

Boslow, Harold M., David Rosenthal, and Lester H. Gliedman. "The Maryland Defective Delinquency Law: Psychiatric Implications for the Treatment of Antisocial Disorders Under the Law." *British Journal of Delinquency*, 10, No. 1 (1959): 5–13.

Boslow, Harold M., David Rosenthal, Arthur Kandel, and Sigmund Manne, "Methods and Experiences in Group Treatment of Defective Delinquents in Maryland." *The Journal of Social Therapy*, Vol. 7, No. 2, (1961):65–75.

Bowman, Anna O.M., and William P. Snyder. "Organizational Acclimatization: An Analysis of the Selective Service System." *Public Administration Quarterly*, 9, No. 2 (Summer 1985): 141–162.

Brawner v. United States, 471 F.2d 969 (D.C. Cir. 1972).

Bromberg, Walter. *Psychiatry Between the Wars, 1918–1945*. Westport, Conn.: Greenwood Press, 1982.

Burns, Tom, "The Comparative Study of Organizations," in *Methods of Organizational Research* (Victor H. Vroom, ed.), Pittsburgh: University of Pittsburgh Press, 1967.

Carney, Francis L. *The Will to Fail*. Unpublished Manuscript, 1985.

———. *Criminality and Its Treatment: The Patuxent Experience*. Malabar, FL: Robert E. Kreiger Publishing Company, Inc., 1989.

Clemmer, Donald. *The Prison Community*. New York: Rinehart, 1958.

Conover, Ted. *Newjack*. New York,: Random House, Inc., 2000.

Contract Research Corporation. The Evaluation of Patuxent Institution Final Report. Belmont, Mass, 1977.

Cullen, Francis T., and Karen E. Gilbert. *Reaffirming Rehabilitation*. Cincinnati, OH: Basic Books, 1982.

DiIulio, John J., Jr. *No Escape: The Future of American Corrections*. Cincinnati, OH: Basic Books, 1991.

Dill, William R. "Environment as an Influence on Managerial Autonomy." *Administrative Science Quarterly*, 2 (March, 1958): 409–433.

DiMaggio, Paul J. "Constructing an Organizational Field as a Professional Project: U.S. Art Museums, 1920–1940," in *The New Institutionalism in Organizational Analysis* (Walter W. Powell and Paul J. DiMaggio, eds.). Chicago: The University of Chicago Press, 1991.

Durham v. United States, 214 F.2d 862 (D.C. Cir. 1954).

Eggleston v. State, 209 Md. 504, 121 A. 2d 698 (1956).

Eldridge, J.E.T., and A.D. Crombie. *A Sociology of Organizations*. New York: International Publications Service, 1975.

Ellenberger, Henri F. *The Discovery of the Unconscious*. New York: Basic Books, 1970.

Evan, William M. "The Organization-Set: Toward a Theory of Interorganizational Relations," in *Approaches to Organizational Design* (James D. Thompson, ed.). Pittsburgh: The University of Pittsburgh Press, 1966.

Feeley, M., and J. Simon. "The New Penology: Notes on the Emerging Strategy of Corrections and its Implications." *Criminology*, vol. 30, no. 4 (1992): 449–474.

Forcese, Dennis P., and Stephen Richer. *Social Research Methods*. Englewood Cliffs, NJ: Prentice-Hall, Inc., 1973.

Foucault, Michael. *Discipline and Punish: The Birth of the Prison*. London: Allen Lane, 1977.

Friedland, Roger, and Robert R. Alford, "Brining Society Back In: Symbols, Practices, and Institutional Contradictions," in *The New Institutionalism in Organizational Analysis* (Walter W. Powell and Paul J. DiMaggio, eds.), Chicago: The University of Chicago Press, 1991.

Frost, Peter J., Larry F. Moore, Meryl Reis Louis, Craig C. Lundberg, and Joanne Martin. *Organizational Culture*. Beverly Hills, CA: Sage Publications, Inc., 1985.

Gabriele, Robert. "Detaining 'Sexual Predators' in the Mental Health System." Washington, DC: National Mental Health Association, 1998.

Garland, David. *Punishment and Modern Society*. Chicago: The University of Chicago Press, 1990.

———. *The Culture of Control*. Chicago: The University of Chicago Press, 2001.

Glaser, B.G., and A. Strauss. *The Discovery of Grounded Theory*. Chicago: Aldine, 1967.

Grob, Gerald N. *The Inner World of American Psychiatry, 1890–1940*. New Brunswick, NJ: Rutgers University Press, 1985.

Halleck, Seymour L., "The Psychiatrist and the Legal Process," in *Law and Change in Modern America* (Joel B. Grossman and Mary H. Grossman, eds.), Pacific Palisades, CA: Goodyear Publishing Company, Inc., 1971.

Hannan, Micheal T., and John Freeman. "The Population Ecology of Organizations." *American Journal of Sociology*, 82 (March 1977), 929–964.

Harrison, Paige M., and Alan Beck. "Prisoners in 2002." U.S. Department of Justice, Bureau of Justice Statistics, July 2003.

Hill, Michael J. *The Sociology of Public Administration*. New York: Crane, Russak, and Co., 1972.

Hood, Roger, and Richard Sparks. *Key Issues in Criminology*. New York: McGraw Hill, 1970.

Jacobs, James B. *Stateville*. Chicago: The University of Chicago Press, 1977.

Katz, Daniel, and Robert L. Kahn. *The Social Psychology of Organizations*. New York: Wiley, 1966.

Kaufmann, Herbert. *Are Government Organizations Immortal?* Washington, DC: Brookings Institution, 1976.

Kimberly, John R. "Environment Constraints and Organizational Structure: A Comparative Analysis of Rehabilitation Organizations." *Administrative Science Quarterly*, 20 (1975): 1–9.

Kimberly, John R., and Robert H. Miles. *The Organizational Life Cycle*. San Francisco: Jossey-Bass, 1980.

Kuhn, Thomas. *The Structure of Scientific Revolutions*. Chicago: The University of Chicago Press, 1962.

Lejins, Peter P. "The Patuxent Experience." *Bulletin of the American Academy of Science and the Law*, 5 (1977): 116–133.

Longmire, Dennis R. "An Empirical Evaluation of a Treatment Program for Habitual Criminal Offienders: The Case of Patuxent Institution." Doctoral thesis submitted and approved at the University of Maryland, 1979.

Lynch, J., and W.J. Sabol. "Prisoner Reentry in Perspective." Washington, DC: The Urban Institute, 2001.

Mahrer, Alvin R., and Leonard Pearson. *Creative Developments in Psychotherapy (Volume I)*. Cleveland: The Press of Case Western Reserve University, 1971.

March, James G., and Herbert Simon. *Organizations*. New York: John Wiley and Sons, Inc., 1958.

Martin, Steve J., and Sheldon Eckland-Olson. *Texas Prisons: The Walls Came Tumbling Down*. Austin, TX: Texas Monthly Press, Inc., 1987.

Maryland Register, Friday, February 23, 1990.

Matson, Scott, and Roxanne Lieb, "Sexual Offender Committtment Laws." Document No. 97-10-1102. Olympia, Washington: Washington State Institute for Public Policy, October 1997.

McDonald, Douglas, William Rhodes, Catherine Conly, Christine Smith, Paul Mahanna, and Valerie Lieter. "Study to Evaluate Patuxent Institution, Volume II: Report of Findings and Technical Appendices." Cambridge, MA: Abt Associates, Inc., December 1990.

McNeil v. Director, Patuxent Institution, No. 71-5144, Supreme Court of the United States, Decided June 19, 1972.

Mead, George H. "The Psychology of Punitive Justice." *American Journal of Sociology,* 23:577–602, March 1918.

Menninger, Karl. "What Is Wrong with Our Prisons?" *Plain Talk* (August 1930): 175–182.

———. "Verdict Guilty—Now What?" *Harper's Magazine* (August 1959).

Merton, Robert K. "The Bearing of Empirical Research upon the Development of Social Theory," *American Sociological Review,* Vol. 5 (1948): 505–555.

———. *Social Theory and Social Structure* (revised edition). New York: The Free Press, 1957.

Meyer, John W., and W. Richard Scott. *Organizational Environments.* Beverly Hills, CA: Sage Publications, 1983.

Morris, Norval. *The Future of Imprisonment.* Chicago: The University of Chicago Press, 1974.

Morris, Norval, and David Rothman. *The Oxford History of the Prison.* New York: Oxford University Press, 1995.

Mukamal, D. "From Hard Time to Full Time: Strategies to Help Move Ex-Offenders from Welfare to Work." Washington, DC: U.S. Department of Labor, Employment and Training Administration, 2001.

Musgrove v. State of Maryland, 241 Md. 521, 217 A. 2d 247 (1966).

Parsons, Talcott. "Suggestions for a Sociological Approach to the Theory of Organizations." *Administrative Science Quarterly,* 1 (1956): 63–85.

———. *Structure and Process in Modern Societies.* New York: The Free Press, 1960.

Patuxent Institution. Annual Report 1969. Jessup, MD: Patuxent Institution, 1969.

———. Annual Report for the Fiscal Years 1973, 1974, 1975. Baltimore: Maryland Department of Public Safety and Correctional Services, 1976.

———. Annual Report Fiscal Year 1981. Baltimore: Maryland Department of Public Safety and Correctional Services, 1981.

———. Annual Report Fiscal Year 1982. Baltimore: Maryland Department of Public Safety and Correctional Services, 1982.

———. Annual Report Fiscal Year 1984. Baltimore: Maryland Department of Public Safety and Correctional Services, 1984.

———. Annual Report Fiscal Year 1986. Baltimore: Maryland Department of Public Safety and Correctional Services, 1987.

———. Annual Report Fiscal Year 1987. Baltimore: Maryland Department of Public Safety and Correctional Services, 1988.

———. Annual Report Fiscal Year 1990. Baltimore: Maryland Department of Public Safety and Correctional Services, 1990.

———. Annual Report Fiscal Year 1999. Baltimore: Maryland Department of Public Safety and Correctional Services, 1999.

———. Annual Report Fiscal Year 2000. Baltimore, Maryland: Maryland Department of Public Safety and Correctional Services, 2000.

Peabody, Robert L., and Francis E. Rourke, "Public Bureaucracies," in *Handbook of Organizations* (James Q. March, ed.). Chicago: Rand McNally and Co., 1965.

Petersilia, Joan, "Parole and Prisoner Reentry in the United States," in *Prisons* (Michael Tonry and Joan Petersilia, eds.), Chicago: The University of Chicago Press, 1999, pp. 479–529.

Pfeffer, Jeffrey. *Organizations and Organization Theory*. Boston: Pitman, 1982.

Pfeffer, Jeffrey, and Gerald R. Salancik. *The External Control of Organizations*. New York: Harper and Row, 1978.

Pike, Ronald L., "The Patuxent Institution: A Study of the Effectiveness of Directive and Non-Directive Treatment Modalities in Treating Defective Delinquents." Unpuplished Masters thesis (believed at the University of Maryland), date unknown (believed circa 1977).

Powell, Walter W., and Paul J. DiMaggio (Eds.). *The New Institutionalism in Organizational Analysis*. Chicago: The University of Chicago Press, 1991.

Rainey, Hal G., Robert W. Backoff, and Charles H. Levine. "Comparing Public and Private Organizations," in *Public Management* (Perry, James L., Kraemer, Kenneth L., eds.), Palo Alto, CA: Mayfield Publishing Co., 1976.

Reiblich Kenneth R., and Herbert H. Hubbard. "An Indeterminate Sentence Law for Defective Delinquents, Research Report No. 29." Baltimore: Legislative Council of Maryland, 1950.

Rotman, Edgardo. "The Failure of Reform," in Morris and Rothman (Eds.). *The Oxford History of the Prison*. New York: Oxford University Press, 1995.

Roy, Robert H. "Dishonored in the Breach: Sabotage of a Good Law." Unpublished paper, circa 1986.

Sas v. Maryland, 334 F. 2d 506 (4th Cir. 1964).

Schwab, Robert C., Gerardo R. Ungson, and Warren B. Brown. "Redefining the Boundary Spanning-Environment Relationship." *Journal of Management*, 2, No. 1 (1985): 75–86.

Selznick, Philip. *TVA and the Grassroots*. Berkeley, CA: University of California Press, 1949.

Shils, Edward, "The Theory of Mass Society," in *Selected Essays by Edward Shils*. Chicago: Center for Legal and Organization Studies, 1970.

Smith, Robert J. *The Psychopath in Society*. New York: Academic Press, 1978.

Stinchcombe, Arthur L. "Social Structure and Organization," in *Handbook of Organizations*, (James G. March, ed.), Chicago: Rand McNally and Co., 1965.

Sykes, Gresham M. *The Society of Captives*. Princeton, NJ: Princeton University Press, 1958.

Thomas, W.I., and F. Znaniecki. *The Polish Peasant in Europe and America*. Chicago: The University of Chicago Press, 1927.

Thompson, James D. *Organizations in Action*. New York: McGraw-Hill, 1967.

Tippet v. State of Maryland, and Director of Patuxent Institution, 436 F. 2d 1153 (4th Cir., 1971).

Tosi, Henry L. *Theories of Organizations*. Chicago: St. Clair Press, 1975.

Travis, Jeremy. "But They All Come Back: Rethinking Prisoner Reentry." Washington, DC: U.S. Department of Justice, National Institute of Justice, 2000.

Travis, Jeremy, A.J. Solomon, and M. Waul. "From Prison to Home: The Dimensions and Consequences of Prisoner Reentry." Washington, DC: The Urban Institute, 2001.

Turner, Barry A. "Some Practical Aspects of Qualitative Data Analysis: One Way of Organizing the Cognitive Processes Associated with the Generation of Grounded Theory." *Quality and Quantity*, 15 (1981): 225–247.

———. "The Use of Grounded Theory for the Qualitative Analysis of Organizational Behavior." *Journal of Management Studies*, 20, No. 3 (1983): 333–348.

Ulman, Joseph N. "Case of Herman Webb Duker, Opinion and Sentence by Joseph N. Ulman, Judge in the Criminal Court of Baltimore City on October 31, 1931."

Wamsley, Gary L., and Mayer N. Zald. *The Political Economy of Public Organizations*. Lexington, MA: D.C. Heath and Co., 1973.

Washington Post, Sunday, November 20, 1988, "15 Years Later, the Pain Lingers." Eugene L. Meyer, Staff Writer, Metro: B1, B5, B7.

———. Tuesday, November 22, 1988, "Holiday Furloughs Cancelled for 21 Patuxent Inmates." Paul Duggan, Staff Writer: A1, A12, A14, A16.

———. Tuesday, November 29, 1988, "Md. Crime Victims Live in the Shadow of Fear." Debbie M. Price: B1, B7.

———. Wednesday, November 30, 1988, "Work Release Is Cut Back at Patuxent." Keith Harriston: D1, D5.

———. Monday, December 5, 1988, "Escaped Rapist Caught in North Carolina." Charles W. Hall: A1, A14.

———. Tuesday, December 6, 1988: D7.

———. Tuesday, January 10, 1989, "Panel Calls for Tightening of Patuxent Release Policies." Howard Schneider. "Schaefer Promises Gentler Session." John Lancaster: Cover, A10, D3.

———. Tuesday, January 26, 1989, "Director of Patuxent Takes Medial Leave." B3.

———. Wednesday, February 15, 1989, "Md. Senate Approves Changes at Patuxent." Howard Schneider: B1, B5.

Weber, Max. *The Theory of Social and Economic Organization* (Translated by A.M. Henderson and Talcott Parsons). New York: The Free Press, 1947.

Wilson, Everett K. "What Counts in the Death or Transformation of an Organization?" *Social Forces*, Vol. 64, No. 2 (December 1985): 259–280.

Yin, Robert K. *Case Study Research.* Beverly Hills, CA: Sage Publications, Inc., 1984.

GENERAL EDITORS

David A. Schultz & Christina DeJong

Studies in Crime and Punishment is a multidisciplinary series that publishes scholarly and teaching materials from a wide range of methodological perspectives and explores sentencing and criminology issues from a single nation or comparative perspective. Subject areas to be addressed in this series include, but will not be limited to: criminology, sentencing and incarceration, policing, law and the courts, juvenile crime, alternative sentencing methods, and criminological research methods.

For additional information about this series or for the submission of manuscripts, please contact:

David A. Schultz
Peter Lang Publishing
Acquisitions Department
275 Seventh Avenue, 28th floor
New York, New York 10001

To order other books in this series, please contact our Customer Service Department:

(800) 770-LANG (within the U.S.)
(212) 647-7706 (outside the U.S.)
(212) 647-7707 FAX

Or browse online by series:

www.peterlangusa.com